JA

Israel and the Arabs

Geoffrey Regan

Published in cooperation with Cambridge University Press
Lerner Publications Company, Minneapolis

LIBRARY OF CONGRESS CATALOGING-IN-PUBLICATION DATA

Regan, Geoffrey
  Israel and the Arabs

  (A Cambridge topic book)
  Includes index.
  Summary: An account of the Middle East conflict
tracing the British rule of Palestine, the founding and
development of the Jewish state of Israel, the growth of
Arab nationalism, and the PLO and the Lebanon War.
  1. Jewish-Arab relations—1917-   —Juvenile literature.
2. Palestine—History—1911-1948—Juvenile literature.
3. Israel—History—Juvenile literature. [1. Jewish-Arab
relations. 2. Palestine History—1917-1948. 3. Israel—
History] I. Title.
DS119.7.R366   1986   956.94'04   85-19843
  ISBN 0-8225-1234-3

This edition first published 1986 by Lerner Publications Company
by permission of Cambridge University Press.

Original edition copyright ©1984 by Cambridge University Press
as part of *The Cambridge Introduction to the History of Mankind: Topic Book*

International Standard Book Number: 0-8225-1234-3
Library of Congress Catalog Card Number: 85-19843

Manufactured in the United States of America

This edition is available exclusively from:
Lerner Publications Company, 241 First Avenue North, Minneapolis, Minnesota 55401

1 2 3 4 5 6 7 8 9 10 97 96 95 94 93 92 91 90 89 88 87 86

Contents

1 The Middle East

A mixture of peoples

At the start of the twentieth century most Europeans thought of the Middle East as a land of fantasy and fairy tale, of Arabian Nights and deserts as vast as seas, of strange customs and fierce, nomadic tribesmen. To Europe's statesmen, however, it was very different: an area of supreme strategic importance.

The Middle East has five thousand years of recorded history. The term can be applied to all the lands from Turkey to Yemen, from Libya to Iran, an area of nine million square kilometres. It has (in 1984) about 140 million people, sometimes – as in the Nile valley – tight-packed, but more often sparsely scattered.

The majority of these people speak some form of the Arabic language, for in their great conquests of the seventh century the Muslims of Arabia carried their religion, culture and language to most of the region. Nevertheless, the whole Middle East is riddled with problems of minority races and religions. Islam tolerated such religious groups as the Coptic Christians of Egypt and the Maronite Christians in Lebanon. Many Jewish communities remained and flourished, scattered through the Arab lands. Minority peoples like Assyrians in Iraq, Circassians in Syria, Armenians in Turkey and neighbouring lands, all pre-date the Muslim conquests. Spread across Turkey, Iraq and Iran is another 'nation without a country', the Kurds, who may number as many as 17 million.

Arabs and Jews in the Middle East

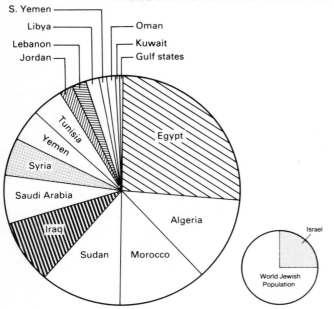

European involvement

Since the fifteenth century the Turkish Ottoman Empire had dominated the Middle East, but by 1900 it was in a state approaching collapse. Over the previous century the Turks had been driven from most of their European possessions. The great European powers, especially Britain, Germany, Russia and France, hoped to gain from Turkey's weakness. They vied with each other to bully or befriend the Turkish sultan and impose their influence in his lands, creating the 'Eastern Question'.

It was Britain that showed the greatest interest, for two main reasons. The Middle East had great importance for Britain's imperial possessions like India and for her trade with the Far East. After the opening of the Suez Canal in 1869, Britain wanted to ensure that its control never fell into the hands of rival powers who might cut her links with her eastern empire. This concern prompted Britain to take control of Egypt in 1882.

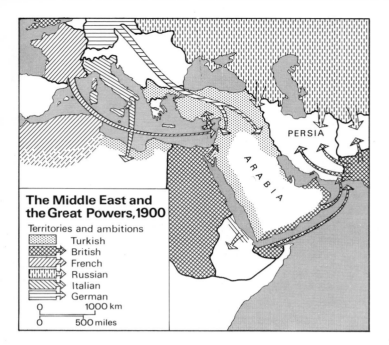

The Middle East and the Great Powers, 1900

Territories and ambitions
- Turkish
- British
- French
- Russian
- Italian
- German

0 ——— 1000 km
0 ——— 500 miles

PERSIA

ARABIA

Britain's second motive was economic. Her navy and merchant fleet were the largest in the world, and dominated seaborne trade. By 1900 the future importance of oil for such ships was already being recognized. The USA and Russia had oil in plenty, and Britain had to choose either to become a customer of her rivals or else find oil of her own. She chose the latter course. In 1901 a Briton won the concession to seek oil in Persia, and by 1909 the Anglo–Persian Oil Company had been set up. The British government took control of the Company in 1914, at the same time securing the main share of Iraq's oil despite strong competition from Germany and the USA. With these strategic and economic interests, Britain regarded the Middle East as her 'sphere of influence'.

Germany also took a keen interest, seeking to win over the Turkish sultan by offering military help. This bore fruit in 1914 when Turkey entered the First World War on the side of Germany. But in 1918 they shared defeat, and thereafter Germany was cut out of the rivalry.

Russia was traditionally ambitious to dominate Turkey and win access to the Mediterranean by way of the Dardanelles. Moreover, Russia's own oilfields in the Caucasus were near the Persian border, and this served to direct her attention towards that country.

France had considered herself the defender of Christians in the Turkish lands ever since the time of the Crusades. French influence was particularly strong in Syria and the Lebanon, where many of her missionaries worked. From about 1860 many Christian Arabs of the Mediterranean coastlands who resented Turkish rule looked towards France to set up and protect a Christian state.

As a result of the First World War, Germany and Russia were, at least temporarily, knocked out of the Middle-Eastern power struggle. Britain and France were left as rivals for the succession to the defeated Turkish Empire. However, there was another contender. The Arab peoples themselves were awakening after centuries of political subjugation.

Arabs and Arabism

The peoples of Libya, Egypt, Sudan, Syria, Palestine, Arabia and Mesopotamia (Iraq) all spoke Arabic, along with other local languages. Most were Muslims, looking back to the great days of Islam. For five hundred years they had been under Turkish overlordship, though throughout the Arab parts of the empire Arab notables held influential positions alongside Turkish governors. In Islam's holy cities in particular, Arab leaders played important parts. In Jerusalem (holy alike for Arabs, Christians and Jews) the *Mufti* (head of the Muslim faith) had great influence. In Mecca, Islam's holiest city, the *Sharif* (local ruler) came from the great family of the Hashemites, directly descended from Mohammed himself.

As Turkey grew weaker, the nationalist ideas that had become popular in Europe spread among educated Arabs. In 1905 Neguib Azouri, a Palestinian Arab living in Paris, put forward the idea of a united Arab state, free of Turkish rule and stretching from the Persian Gulf to the Suez Canal. His book was called *The Awakening of the Arab Nation*, but few Arabs responded to the call, for there were many differences and divisions among the Arab peoples and without a leader and modern weapons they could not hope to throw off Turkish control.

In 1908 a revolution in Turkey brought the 'Young Turks' into power at Constantinople. They hoped to provide the crumbling empire with strong government from the centre. Many Arabs were alarmed by the prospect of firmer Turkish control; the power they had enjoyed under slack government might disappear. The Sharif of Mecca, Hussein ibn Ali, and his sons were particularly alarmed, and the Hashemite family saw themselves as champions of the Arab cause within the Turkish Empire. If they were to end Turkish rule, they needed a powerful ally.

The outbreak of war in 1914 gave them their chance. When Turkey entered the war beside Germany the British High Commissioner in Cairo, Sir Henry MacMahon, also sought an ally. In a series of letters to Hussein, and especially one sent on 24 October 1915, Sir Henry promised Britain's help in setting up a united Arab state in return for Arab military action against the Turks. The area to be included in the proposed Arab state was left rather vague. It certainly included most of the Turkish province of Syria, and Hussein naturally assumed that this included Palestine, which was part of that province. The dispute over Palestine can be traced from this point.

On the strength of this promise the Sharif and his sons, Ali, Feisal and Abdullah, led a rising against the Turks. They assumed that they would rule the new state. Others thought differently, such as Ibn Saud, leader of the austere Wahabi sect of desert Arabs. The British supplied Hussein with money, weapons and a few soldiers. One young officer and mystic, named T.E. Lawrence, captured the hearts of the Arabs by his commitment to their cause and won fame for himself as 'Lawrence of Arabia'.

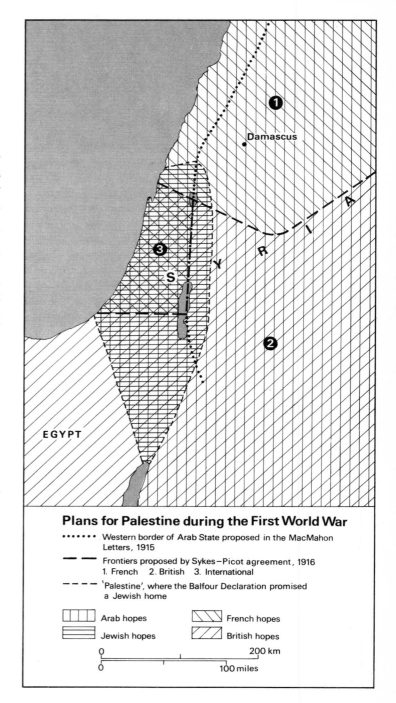

Plans for Palestine during the First World War

••••••• Western border of Arab State proposed in the MacMahon Letters, 1915

— — Frontiers proposed by Sykes–Picot agreement, 1916
1. French   2. British   3. International

– – – – 'Palestine', where the Balfour Declaration promised a Jewish home

Arab hopes   French hopes

Jewish hopes   British hopes

0   200 km

0   100 miles

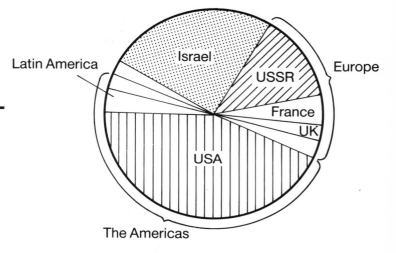

Latin America · Israel · USSR · Europe · France · UK · USA · The Americas

Abdullah ibn Hussein, 1880–1951, son of the Sharif of Mecca, was his father's agent in seeking British help for a rising against Turkish rule. He led an Arab army in the desert war. With British backing, set himself up as Emir (Commander) of the Arab tribes in the land later called Transjordan. King when British Mandate ended, 1946. Took over non-Israeli Palestine, 1949, becoming King of Jordan. Assassinated in Jerusalem by Arabs who thought him a traitor.

While MacMahon was negotiating with Hussein ibn Ali, the British and French governments were discussing their plans for the post-war division of the Middle East. In 1916 they signed the Sykes–Picot agreement to define their 'spheres of influence' once the Turks had been beaten. They agreed to protect and recognize an independent Arab state, but neither wished to grant the Arabs independence too soon. France, because of her traditional religious and trading links, was eager to maintain a foothold in Lebanon and Syria. Britain was anxious to protect the Suez Canal and her oil interests in the Persian Gulf. Thus, in spite of her promise to the Arabs, Britain was determined to strengthen her hold in the Middle East. Arab independence would just have to wait.

Jews and Zionism

The story of the Jews is a complex and tragic one. Most of Israel's four million people are Jews, yet there are three times as many Jews outside Israel. Of these, nearly six million live in the USA. There are two million in the USSR, and many again in western Europe, despite the fact that over five million European Jews died under the Nazis.

Judaism is one of the world's great religions. A Jew is anyone who holds that faith, and their common faith binds all Jews together, wherever they live and whatever tongue they speak. Some Jews, and many of their enemies, think of the Jews as a separate race, descended from those driven out of Palestine by the Romans in the great *diaspora*, or scattering, of two thousand years ago. They have an ancient language, the Hebrew once used in Palestine; but few outside Israel today understand more than a few words or use it except in religious practices. With the exception of their ancient holy books, the Jews' language and literature is linked more closely to the lands where they live now than to those of Palestine or of other Jews, like the Yiddish (derived from German) spoken by most European Jews. In two thousand years, Palestinian blood has mingled with that of the peoples among whom Jews settled, while some European Jews, it is thought, may in fact descend from the Khazars, a semi-nomadic Turko-Finnish people of Southern Russia who were converted to Judaism in the seventh century and settled down in their new faith to become merchants and city-dwellers.

But Jews everywhere look upon those Jews of Palestine whose story is told in the Bible as their true forebears, the founders of their faith. For all Jews Jerusalem, sometimes called Zion, is the city of God, where the great rulers David and Solomon built the first temples of Judaism.

Partly because they clung so strongly to this tradition, and to their own special way of life, with customs, dress, diet, calendar and festivals brought from their homeland, the Jews often found themselves distrusted by the people among whom they lived. They seemed deliberately foreign, outsiders, secretive. There were other reasons for the Jews' unpopularity. Good Christians of the Middle Ages hated them as the people who had betrayed Jesus. Poor, honest, working men envied their wealth, for while the Church sternly forbade Christians to lend money for profit, it seemed that Jewish money-lenders and bankers were allowed to grow rich at the expense of others. The growth of industry in the nineteenth century sharpened attitudes; successful Jewish merchants and bankers like the Rothschilds grew even wealthier, while factory workers crowded in ugly cities and farmers struggling to pay the rent felt their poverty somehow resulted from the selfish greed of others.

In this period of economic and social struggle the ideas of men like Marx and Nietzsche were very influential. However, it was Darwin's scientific theories of human evolution and natural selection which were twisted by unscrupulous people to appeal to the frustrated urban populations of central and eastern Europe. They argued that mankind was divided into races, some better fitted than others to survive and lead. The Jews, it was claimed, were a different race, carefully preserving their separateness, unclean and Asiatic. Like the Arab peoples, Jews were 'Semites', distinct from the 'Caucasians' or 'Aryans' among whom they lived.

Attacks on Jews, 'anti-semitism', grew more violent in the 1880s and 1890s. In France, in the 1890s, patriots led a popular attack on the Jewish Captain Dreyfus, accused of spying. In Germany and Austria, clever politicians like George von Schönerer and Karl Lueger won support by stirring up anti-semitic feeling; their ideas and successes influenced the young Adolf Hitler. However, the most violent attacks on Jews occurred in Russia. There, five million Jews were restricted to an area known as the 'Pale of Settlement'. After the assassination of Tsar Alexander II in 1881, Russia's rulers from time to time made use of the unpopular Jews as scapegoats, a safety valve for the discontent of Russia's impoverished masses. Local authorities, and even the Tsar's ministers, encouraged poor folk to let off steam by attacking and murdering local Jews in savage *pogroms*; sometimes the Tsar's soldiers joined in. Hundreds of Jews died, and many thousands left their homes to seek safety in Britain or America. Some, with financial help from Lord Rothschild, made their way to Palestine. There, land was bought and Jewish farming villages were set up.

In western Europe many Jews, like the Viennese journalist Theodor Herzl, reacted forcefully to persecution. Herzl believed that the Jews, forced for centuries to live among alien people, would never feel safe. The answer he proposed was to return to the land from which the Jews had been driven, to Zion. There they would make a new Jewish homeland, even a new country. Herzl published his book, *The Jewish State*, in 1896. Next year, he called a conference at Basle of 206 delegates to form the World Zionist Organization, with its headquarters at Vienna. The Zionists looked back to the great days of the kings of Israel, when Mount Zion had been the fortress of Jerusalem. Only in this way could they draw together all the widely different Jewish communities. They chose for their

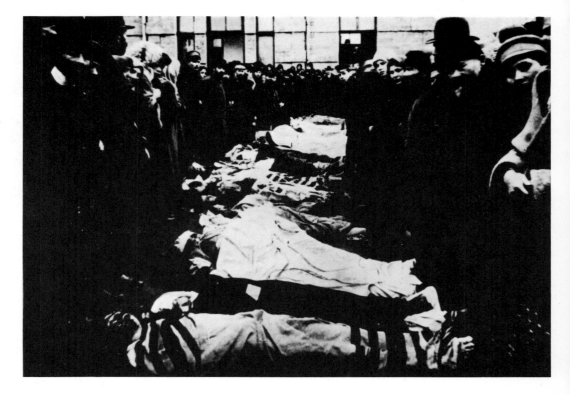

(below) **Israeli flag**
(right) **Menorah**

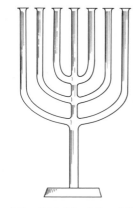

emblems the six-pointed star known as 'The Shield of David' and the seven-branched candelabrum of the Temple, the *menorah*.

Herzl hoped at first to obtain permission from the Turks for the Jews to make their homeland in Palestine. Failing in this, he approached Britain for help. The British were sympathetic, and offered two alternative sites, neither exactly practicable, for a Jewish homeland. The Jews rejected both, Sinai because of lack of water and Uganda because they had no historic links with Africa. Nevertheless, the idea of a Jewish home had been launched, and the Zionists had made important friends in Britain. After Herzl died, Dr Chaim Weizmann, an emigré Russian scientist who had become a naturalised Briton, became one of their principal leaders. He was known and respected by leading British politicians.

Between 1904 and 1914, 40,000 Jews migrated to Palestine, mainly from Russia, swelling the Jewish population to over 80,000. This was only a small fraction, perhaps about one-eighth, of Palestine's total population, but the Jews were a very active minority. The 'new' settlers were very different from the native Jews, whose families had been there for centuries and who fitted easily into the Palestinian way of life. The new Jews were European in background and outlook, fired by

Tel Aviv, 'the Hill of Spring', was founded by Jews in 1909 as a garden suburb of Jaffa. Here, the founders cast lots for their shares of the empty site. Tel Aviv soon grew into a thriving modern city, the business capital of Israel.

Theodor Herzl, 1860–1904, son of a wealthy Jewish merchant of Budapest, became a lawyer and writer. As a journalist in Paris, witnessed anti-semitisim during the Dreyfus affair, and concluded Jews must have a home of their own. His book The Jewish State, 1896, laid down aims for the Zionist movement. Convened Basle Conference, 1897, founding the World Zionist Organization to seek a homeland for Jews in Palestine.

Dr Chaim Weizmann, 1874– 1952, was born in western Russia. He studied at German universities, becoming chemistry lecturer at Manchester and later a leading British scientist during the 1914–18 war. An active Zionist, his friendship with government ministers helped win their support for Balfour's Declaration. President of World Zionist Organization 1917–30, 1935–46. Worked closely with Britain to secure a Jewish home, sometimes clashing with more extreme Zionists. 1949, Israel's first president. His Zionism was not just political; he sought to build Jewish education and culture as well as a Jewish state.

religious enthusiasm and determination to build a new homeland. Theirs was a pioneering vision; hard work would restore the 'land flowing with milk and honey' that had been neglected since their forefathers' exile.

In the countryside Jewish farms and settlements spread. The *moshav* was for smallholders, the *kibbutz* a communal, co-operative settlement. The first kibbutz was set up in 1909 at Degania, in swampy, malaria-ridden land by the Sea of Galilee, the only kind available to immigrants. In the towns, Jews organized trade unions and later joined in the *Histadrut* or Federation of Jewish Labour. Kibbutzim and trade unions began to break down the differences between immigrants from so many different backgrounds, speaking Russian, Polish, Ukranian, Yiddish and a score of other languages. A Jewish newspaper helped the resurgence of Hebrew, to give a greater sense of unity. But the language of the Old Testament lacked words for modern objects, and additions had to be invented for items like socks, rifles and trains.

These activities began to alarm the Arabs, who had lived for centuries in harmony with their Jewish neighbours. To the Arab peasant the new Jews were alien, with their education, their skills and their modern technology. The peaceful co-existence of Jew and Arab was about to be shattered.

The Balfour Declaration

When war came in 1914 the Turkish rulers of Palestine became Britain's enemies. Weizmann and other Zionists saw fresh hopes for British help. There was a sympathetic British

Jew, Herbert Samuel, in the government. David Lloyd George, who became prime minister in 1916, and Arthur Balfour, his foreign secretary, were known to be friendly to the Jewish cause. In 1917 they had good political reasons for a generous gesture to the Jews. For one thing, they wanted to please the many Jewish voters in the USA, which at last entered the war in that year. They would also please President Wilson, for the Zionist claim seemed in accordance with his ideals of national self-determination. In Russia the 1917 revolution brought Jews like Trotsky to the fore, and they might be encouraged to continue fighting on Britain's side. Finally, it seemed important to have friendly Jews in Palestine as a buffer to protect Egypt and Suez from the French in Syria.

On 2 November 1917 Arthur Balfour wrote a letter to Lord Rothschild, as the leading British Jew, which contained this famous declaration:

> His Majesty's Government view with favour the establishment in Palestine of a national home for the Jewish people, and will use their best endeavours to facilitate the achievement of this object, it being clearly understood that nothing shall be done which may prejudice the civil and religious rights of existing non-Jewish communities in Palestine or the rights and political status enjoyed by Jews in any other country.

This document has, since 1917, aroused great controversy, and Britain has been accused of offering the same land to two different groups and betraying her earlier promises to the Arabs. The Declaration was carefully worded, and the British could argue that they had only offered a home *in* Palestine, where Jews had already lived peaceably alongside Arabs for centuries. There was no intention that they should take over the whole of Palestine.

This was what the Zionists hoped ultimately to do, however, and the Palestinian Arabs understood their intentions. The Zionists knew that the misfortunes of European Jews were a result of being in the minority everywhere. They intended to achieve a majority in Palestine as speedily as possible, which would certainly 'prejudice the civil rights' of the Arabs living there. This was clearly Zionist policy from the outset. If Britain could not stop it, some Arab leaders determined that they would.

Key events

1896	Herzl's book *The Jewish State*
1897	World Zionist Organization
1908	Young Turk revolution
1915	MacMahon letters promised an Arab state
1916	Sykes–Picot agreement
1917	Balfour Declaration

2 British rule in Palestine 1919–45

The Mandate

When the war ended it seemed that hopes for a peaceful settlement of Palestine might be realised, for in January 1919, Dr Weizmann and the Emir Feisal agreed to the terms of the Balfour Declaration. 'We wish the Jews a most hearty welcome home,' wrote Feisal, adding that there was room for both Arabs and Jews in the Greater Syria he hoped to rule. As the new lords of the Arab lands, the Hashemites would be generous to their fellow Semites.

This atmosphere was not to last for long. Hashemite hopes of leading a united Arab world were soon dashed, for they clashed with the plans of Britain and France and alarmed other Arab rulers. Sharif Hussein, called 'King of the Arabs', ruled briefly in Hejaz with his eldest son Ali. In 1924 they were driven out by Ibn Saud's fierce Wahabi warriors from the desert, who united most of Arabia under the Saudi dynasty. The Sharif's son Feisal had no sooner been acclaimed King of Syria (including Palestine) in 1920 than the French arrived to expel him. The British allowed him to become King of Iraq, as Mesopotamia was now known, while his brother Abdullah had to be satisfied with the desert lands of eastern Palestine, then called Transjordan. Both remained for the time being under British supervision.

Convinced that, despite their claims and Allied promises, the Arabs were not ready for independence, Britain and France went ahead with their planned partition of the Middle East. Turkey's conquerors met at San Remo in April, 1920, to award themselves mandates under the League of Nations and take over the former Turkish Empire. France took Syria (including Lebanon), Britain took Mesopotamia and Palestine; Britain also kept her control of Egypt.

In taking up her Palestine mandate Britain agreed to implement the Balfour Declaration. Soon, despite the Weizmann–Feisal agreement, she was facing trouble. The Zionists were determined to fill Palestine with Jewish immigrants as soon as possible. They set up a 'Jewish Agency' to help migrants and to find them land and jobs. Though they were treated sympathetically by Britain's High Commissioner, Sir Herbert Samuel, they found him determined to be fair to the Palestine Arabs.

The Arabs feared that the influx of European Jews would dispossess them of their land. The newcomers had more money and better education. They were able to buy up Arab estates and businesses, to succeed and prosper where Arabs had only been able to scrape a bare living. This was good for the country as a whole, but it aroused Arab resentment. They distrusted Samuel, who was a Jew. Would he not, they argued, be bound to favour the Zionists against the Arabs? The answer was most definitely not. Although sympathetic towards Zionism, Samuel went to great pains to be impartial in the dispute between Arab and Jew. Like most Jews throughout the world, he was loyal firstly to the land of his

Sir Herbert (Lord) Samuel, 1870–1963, was born in Liverpool to a wealthy Jewish banking family. Became a leading Liberal politician, and held Cabinet posts in the 1906–16 Liberal governments. During the war, urged his colleagues to provide a Jewish home in Palestine. High Commissioner for Palestine, 1920–25. Wise and moderate, he developed Palestine's economy and sought harmony between Arab and Jew.

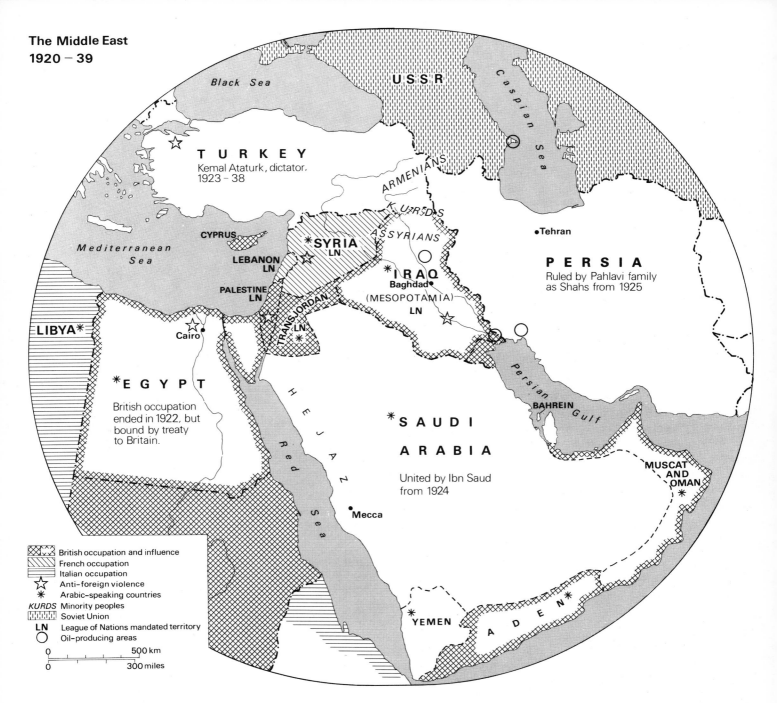

The Middle East
1920 – 39

Black Sea

USSR

Caspian Sea

T U R K E Y
Kemal Ataturk, dictator,
1923 – 38

ARMENIANS

KURDS

ASSYRIANS

CYPRUS

Mediterranean Sea

LEBANON
LN

PALESTINE
LN

SYRIA
LN

IRAQ
Baghdad
(MESOPOTAMIA)
LN

•Tehran

P E R S I A
Ruled by Pahlavi family
as Shahs from 1925

TRANSJORDAN
LN

LIBYA

Cairo

EGYPT
British occupation
ended in 1922, but
bound by treaty
to Britain.

Red Sea

H E J A Z

**S A U D I
A R A B I A**
United by Ibn Saud
from 1924

•Mecca

Persian Gulf

BAHREIN

**MUSCAT
AND
OMAN**

YEMEN

A D E N

British occupation and influence
French occupation
Italian occupation
Anti-foreign violence
Arabic-speaking countries
KURDS Minority peoples
Soviet Union
LN League of Nations mandated territory
Oil-producing areas

0   500 km
0   300 miles

13

birth; and he was in Palestine as representative of Britain, not of the Jews.

In the towns and villages of Palestine, Arab–Jewish relations quickly worsened, leading to an outbreak of violence in Jerusalem, known as the 'Passover Riots', in April 1920. Jewish shops were wrecked, while six Jews were killed and 200 wounded. The Jewish response to the failure of the British government and police to keep order was to form their own Defence Force, *Haganah*. When fresh violence broke out in 1921 Haganah struck back. Scores were killed on each side, tales of atrocities began to circulate and bitterness grew between Jews and Arabs.

The British government made the first of many attempts to calm Arab fears and satisfy Jewish demands. Winston Churchill, Britain's Colonial Secretary, visited Palestine in 1921, and next year issued a 'White Paper' outlining the government's plans. The Jews might develop their own religious and cultural centre in Palestine; Churchill was impressed by the way in which they were already doing much to restore prosperity and progress to an underpopulated and backward land. But there would be no Jewish political authority. Nor could Palestine have an elective government or independence, as the Arabs wanted, for the Arab majority would simply forbid future Jewish immigration. Arab and Jew, the British hoped, would co-operate to build a new Palestine.

In many ways these were sensible suggestions, yet both Arabs and Jews felt that Britain was going back on promises. Meanwhile, Zionist plans were enlarged and British attempts to limit immigration undermined by events in Europe and America. Jews fleeing persecution in Poland and Russia found that the land to which so many had gone before was no longer open to them, for from 1924 the USA severely restricted immigration.

Britain feared an Arab backlash if Jewish numbers were not kept down. And now the Palestinian Arabs found a leader:

Haj Amin al Husseini, once a Turkish army officer, was appointed by Samuel as Mufti (or chief Muslim lawgiver) of Jerusalem. It turned out to be a disastrous choice. The Mufti incited his followers to attack Jews and eventually preached *Jihad*, Holy War, against all unbelievers in Palestine. When violence broke out again in 1929 hundreds of Jews were killed, including 67 massacred in the town of Hebron. Isolated Jewish settlements were wiped out by Arab attacks, for British troops were too few to give protection and Arab police often would not. As a result, more frightened and embittered Jews became Zionists and supported Haganah, working actively for a state of their own.

Haj Amin al Husseini, 1893–1974, was born in Jerusalem and became an officer in the Turkish army, 1910. 1921, appointed Mufti (lawgiver) and President of the Muslim Council, leader of Palestine's Muslims. Became an outspoken and violent enemy of Zionists, Jews, and British administrators. 1936, called General Strike and Jihad (Holy War). Fled from the British to Lebanon, later to Germany as guest of Hitler. 1945, in Egypt, but never regained political leadership. His violent tactics persuaded Britain to limit Jewish settlement in 1939, but ended chance of British–Arab alliance against Israel.

Jewish immigrants to Palestine–Israel

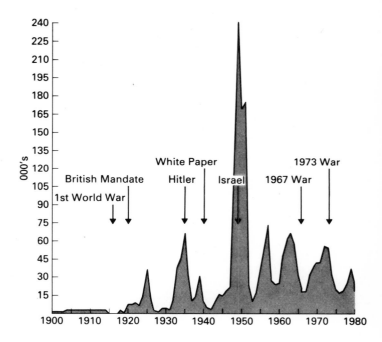

Partition plans

The rise of Adolf Hitler in Germany had an immediate effect on Jewish immigration into Palestine. Although some German Jews stayed, in the mistaken belief that the Nazis would become more moderate once they had gained power, others chose flight.

The British tried to keep control of immigration, but many Jews landed illegally by night, or were smuggled over the borders from neighbouring states. This influx brought Jewish numbers up to a third of those of the Arabs, with the possibility that eventually Jews would outnumber Arabs. It triggered the violent Arab Revolt of 1936–39. The Mufti preached open rebellion and called for guerilla warfare against the British authorities. A general strike was followed by a campaign of murders, attacks on trains, and sabotage. The Jews, often targets of the violence, retaliated through their defence force, Haganah, and the new and more ruthless 'National Military Organization', *Irgun Zvai Leumi*.

The British took vigorous military action to quell the revolt, and the Mufti and his fellow leaders were driven into exile. In three years of fighting 1,785 people were killed, including 517 Jews.

Against this background of violence and challenge to authority, Britain sought a new solution to the problem of

Palestine's future. A Royal Commission, headed by Lord Peel, was sent out, and reported in July 1937. This time the message was clear, and very different from that of previous British enquiries; the situation was out of hand. The Report spoke of 'an irrepressible conflict' between Arab and Jew because of the Arab desire for national independence and their hatred of the idea of a Jewish national home. It was impossible to reconcile both interests with the Mandate. The only solu-

The Jews in Palestine

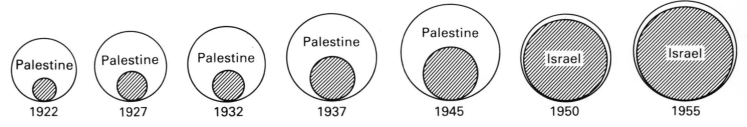

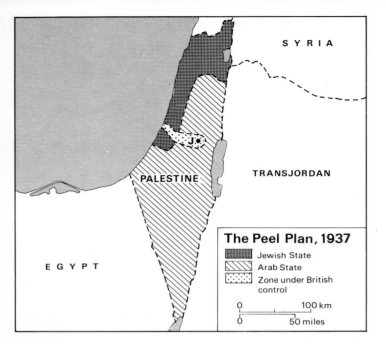

The Peel Plan, 1937
- ▓ Jewish State
- ▨ Arab State
- ░ Zone under British control

0   100 km
0   50 miles

SYRIA

TRANSJORDAN

PALESTINE

EGYPT

tion, said the Peel Report, was to partition Palestine between Arab and Jew.

Partition would have many dangers. It would mean that many Jewish settlements must come under Arab rule (for they were widely scattered) while even more Arab farmers and town-dwellers would be left in the Jewish lands. Unless there were firm British control of the handover, it would lead to almost certain conflict, since each side believed itself entitled to rule all Palestine. But the alternative was continued anarchy, as Arabs fought for immediate majority rule and Jews pressed on towards the time when they would be the majority.

The Peel plan pointed a way forward, but like any compromise solution it satisfied no one. Most Jews accepted those parts that offered them a state of some kind; but the British government soon dropped it as impracticable. Nevertheless, the growing danger of war in Europe forced Britain to try again to calm the Palestine situation in a way that would not alienate Arabs and endanger Persian Gulf oil supplies. A new White Paper was issued on 17 May 1939 laying down a fresh policy. There was to be an independent Palestine within ten years, with a power-sharing government to safeguard the interests of both Arabs and Jews. Meanwhile, Jewish immigration was to be limited to 15,000 a year for five years, with no more thereafter unless the Arabs agreed. Though Jews were allowed to purchase land, there would be no Jewish state.

Zionist leaders claimed that Britain was abandoning the Balfour Declaration. Hopes of achieving a Jewish state with British help seemed to be disappearing, so many turned instead to the United States. But three months after the White Paper the Second World War broke out.

The Second World War

The Second World War transformed the Middle East. Britain held fast to her position there, though she had to fight Italians and Germans in Libya and Egypt, the Vichy French in Syria, and pro-German Arab nationalists in Iraq and elsewhere. When victory came in 1945 Britain seemed enormously powerful, and her forces dominated the whole region. Even the independence of India only strengthened Britain's interest in the Middle East, which became a vital base for the Western powers in the Cold War against the Russian threat from the north. War had underlined the vital importance of the region's oil, and production in all the Arab states mounted rapidly. If ever these supplies were threatened, as they were during disturbances in Iran in 1951, then British troops stood ready to take action.

The Arabs emerged strengthened and changed by the upheavals of war. For the most part, their rulers had backed Britain, and at the end of the war many had joined in declaring war on Germany to gain seats in the United Nations and a voice in world affairs. In 1944 they sank many of their old quarrels and planned an Arab League, which came into existence with its headquarters in Cairo in the following year. The League brought together Egypt, Syria, Lebanon, Iraq, Transjordan, Saudi Arabia and later, Yemen. It encouraged co-operation for scientific, economic and cultural progress between these poor and underdeveloped states, newly freed from Western domination; but there were too many disagreements to make much progress towards political unity.

On one subject the members of the Arab League were agreed: Palestine. There, increasing violence brought extremist leaders to the fore. One of these, the tough trade-union leader David Ben-Gurion, replaced the moderate Chaim Weizmann as Zionism's principal spokesman. In May 1942 he persuaded some six hundred leading American Jews, meeting at the Biltmore Hotel in New York, to back Zionist demands for unlimited immigration to build a Jewish Palestine. Ben-Gurion hoped to flood Palestine with Jews escaping from Nazi Europe, and he was prepared to fight the British and their White Paper to get them in.

New militancy was apparent in the activities of Jewish terrorists, whose violence went far beyond Ben-Gurion's. A fanatical young poet formed the 'Stern Gang' to assassinate anyone standing in the way of Zionist aims; in 1944 they murdered Britain's minister in the Middle East, Lord Moyne. Abraham Stern died in a shoot-out with the police, but Irgun Zvai Leumi, now led by Menachem Begin, adopted similar ruthless tactics. Their methods shocked many Jews, but they effectively focussed attention in Britain and America on the demands of the most outspoken Zionists.

Of even more importance to the Zionist cause was the fate of Europe's Jews during the war. When the full story was told of how five or six million Jews had died in the Nazi 'Holocaust', Jewish people everywhere came round to believing that the best hope for the future was an independent Jewish state. There, future Jewish refugees might find safety and there they could defend themselves against all dangers. Many Jews had tried to be good Germans, and had not resisted Hitler's government, but they had been destroyed

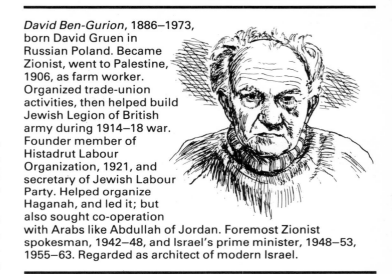

David Ben-Gurion, 1886–1973, born David Gruen in Russian Poland. Became Zionist, went to Palestine, 1906, as farm worker. Organized trade-union activities, then helped build Jewish Legion of British army during 1914–18 war. Founder member of Histadrut Labour Organization, 1921, and secretary of Jewish Labour Party. Helped organize Haganah, and led it; but also sought co-operation with Arabs like Abdullah of Jordan. Foremost Zionist spokesman, 1942–48, and Israel's prime minister, 1948–53, 1955–63. Regarded as architect of modern Israel.

nevertheless. They must never allow another enemy such an opportunity, never compromise. They must strike first and hardest. In addition, Jewish suffering won them world-wide sympathy. Many governments felt guilty that they had in the past done too little to help these persecuted people. After such terrible treatment, the atrocities of Stern and Begin seemed understandable. Zionist propaganda seized every opportunity to exploit this sympathy, and painted Britons and Arabs as successors to the SS and the Gestapo.

Key events

1920	British Mandate of Palestine. Jewish–Arab riots. Emir Feisal expelled from Syria by France.
1922	Churchill White Paper suggests joint Arab–Jewish progress
1933	Hitler came to power in Germany
1936–39	Arab Revolt
1937	Peel Report proposed partition of Palestine
1939	White paper restricted immigration and proposed joint government
1942	Biltmore Hotel program for a Zionist Palestine
1940–45	Nazi massacres of European Jews
1945	Arab League formed

3 The foundation of Israel 1945–49

Britain and the United Nations

Ernest Bevin, who became Britain's foreign secretary in 1945, hoped to solve Palestine's problems along the lines proposed in the White Paper before the war: with some kind of shared government and no great influx of Jews to upset the Arab majority. But he found himself lost in a maze of conflicting demands.

Palestinian Arabs argued passionately that their country should not be made a dumping ground for Jews that Europe did not want, that Arabs should not become the innocent victims with whom the West atoned for its sins against Jews. Any renewal of Arab violence would endanger both Britain's vital oil supplies and the huge military base she was establishing in Palestine as the centre of her Middle East and Cold War strategy. Though Arab rulers such as the Hashemite kings of Iraq and Transjordan still found Britain's support useful, many Arabs distrusted Britain as an imperialist power, still seeking to dominate the Middle East. So did the rest of the world. France was bitter because Britain had scored in their old Middle-Eastern rivalry by encouraging the Syrians to get rid of the French in 1945. President Truman of the United States was under pressure from American Jews to support the Biltmore Hotel program, while his own State Department was anxious to keep on friendly terms with the Arab countries. At one moment he urged Britain to admit 100,000 Jewish refugees immediately, regardless of the consequences; at another, he rejected the idea of an independent Jewish state. His interventions caused trouble, but he was not willing for the United States to be drawn into the dispute.

Meanwhile the miserable survivors of Europe's death camps, for whom entry to the peaceful and prosperous USA was still restricted, found Zionist enthusiasts urging them to demand admittance to troubled Palestine.

Bevin, exasperated by outspoken Zionist propaganda, was unable to act effectively. The Jews abandoned all restraint, knowing that most of the world was on their side. Haganah worked with terrorist groups in attacking British bases and soldiers. In July 1946 Begin's Irgun blew up a wing of the King David Hotel in Jerusalem occupied by British military headquarters. Ninety-one people were killed, including both Arabs and Jews. British commanders used harsh words and rough methods in reply, but only succeeded in antagonising more Jews and giving them evidence for their propaganda campaign.

Finding a solution beyond him, Bevin turned to Truman for help. A joint Commission of Inquiry, six Americans and six Britons, visited Palestine, Arab states and European camps, before reporting in April 1946 that the 100,000 refugees in urgent need should be allowed immediate entry as Truman had asked. Apart from that, the Commission could only suggest continuation of the British Mandate, to preserve some kind of order. This joint policy satisfied no one, for both Arabs and Jews were now convinced that they must secure control of Palestine by force when British authority crumbled. As the violence grew, and law and order collapsed, Bevin decided it was time to relinquish responsibility for Palestine. On 14 February 1947 he announced that Britain would refer the problem to the United Nations.

The UN promptly set up a Special Commission on Palestine (UNSCOP), with representatives from 11 member states. It was subjected to skilfully organized propaganda from the Zionists, and boycotted completely by the Arabs, who felt it had no right to interfere in their land. It produced a very complex plan for partition, approved by the UN General Assembly in November 1947. Palestine was to be carved into three separate Jewish and three Arab parts, with Jerusalem under international control.

The Jews accepted the UN plan, for on the whole the proposals favoured them and provided a state they could call their own. The Arabs rejected it, for their leaders were now deter-

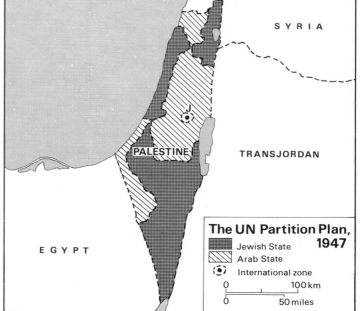

The 'Exodus' incident occurred during the UN visit to Palestine. Haganah bought an American ship, renamed it 'Exodus 1947', packed it with 4,500 refugees, and tried to land them at Haifa. The British, afraid of Arab reaction, returned the passengers to France whence they had come. When they refused to land there, they were taken to British-occupied Germany and forcibly landed. Zionist propaganda scored a great success with heart-rending stories of their suffering, portraying the British authorities as heartless.

The UN Partition Plan, 1947

Jewish State
Arab State
International zone

0   100 km
0   50 miles

mined to use superior numbers and Arab League support to win a military victory. Their reaction was not surprising for statistically the UN solution seemed grossly unfair:

	JEWS	ARABS AND OTHERS
Population (1947)	608,000	1,327,000
Land owned (1947)	10.6%	89.4%
Territory allotted by UN plan	56.5%	43.5%

As soon as the UN approved the plan, Britain announced her intention of quitting Palestine as quickly as possible, by 15 May 1948, leaving the Arabs and Jews to implement partition themselves. At once each side set about frightening their opponents away from the lands they claimed, attacking isolated villages with terrible ferocity. Many Jewish settlers were killed in the first few days, as British troops and officials were pulled out. Then the Jewish terrorist groups retaliated. Their reprisals reached a peak when Irgun massacred 254 vil-

David Ben-Gurion, architect of the new state, declares Israel's independence at Tel Aviv on 14 May 1948.

lagers, mostly women and children, at Deir Yassin in April 1948. This atrocity shocked many Jews, and Ben-Gurion was quick to condemn those responsible; but Haganah nevertheless worked closely with the extremist groups as the Jews closed ranks. The Arabs struck back in turn, ambushing a convoy of supplies and medical aid on the Jerusalem road and killing many doctors and nurses. But Jewish terror proved more effective. Arab villagers under threat left their homes and fled. Jewish villagers, having nowhere to flee to, either stood and fought or died.

By the end of 1948 half a million Arabs had abandoned their homes. The Palestinian refugee problem was born.

The new state

'If you will it, it is no dream.' These words of Theodor Herzl must have been in the minds of many Jews when, on 14 May 1948, the last British High Commissioner left Palestine. That day David Ben-Gurion proclaimed the new state, to be called Israel after the Biblical kingdom, with Chaim Weizmann as president. After fifty years the Zionist dream had come to pass; those Jews who wanted one had a homeland of their own.

A new country had emerged in the Middle East, and it soon enjoyed spectacular success. Russia welcomed Israel as a fellow socialist state and, moreover, one which denied Britain a military base in the Eastern Mediterranean. The United States was also quick to recognize the new state, and from many parts of the world came offers of help. Israel desperately needed such help. She wanted weapons and the money to buy them, surrounded as she was by the implacable hatred of the Arab world.

In this crisis situation Ben-Gurion sent his colleague Golda Meir on a fund-raising trip to the USA. Arriving in New York with a mere ten dollars in her purse, she proved so effective an advocate of the Jewish cause that a month later she returned home with fifty million dollars donated by wealthy American Jews. In this single act, declared Ben-Gurion, Golda Meir had ensured the survival of the new state. She had also made clear Israel's dependence on American money, demonstrating to resentful Arab states and the suspicious Communist world that the United States had now intruded into the Middle East to establish a new base of its own.

Throughout the world Jewish agents had been purchasing arms. At home, the Jews overcame their internal differences to face their Arab rivals. Begin's Irgun followers, who sought to overthrow Ben-Gurion's government and demanded the whole territory of 'Eretz Israel', the ancient kingdom, were crushed by Haganah commandos in a fierce fight at Tel Aviv. Israel was now ready to meet the threats of her Arab neighbours.

The Palestine War 1948–49

When the armies of Syria, Transjordan, Lebanon, Iraq and Egypt came to the aid of the Palestinian Arabs on 15 May 1948, the Jews seemed to be outnumbered three to one and their destruction appeared certain. But the picture was not as black as it may seem. The Jews had an advantage in weapons, for thousands of rifles and some aircraft had arrived, bought from Czechoslovakia with American money. They had able and determined leaders with a common aim, facing an unco-ordinated two-pronged invasion. Above all they had the will to win. Theirs was a people's army, fighting for the country

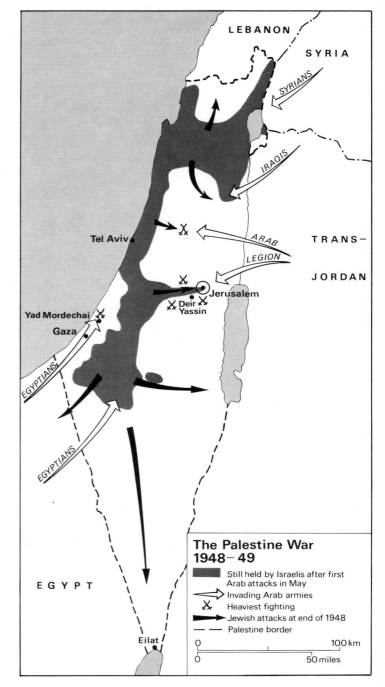

The Palestine War 1948–49

- ▓ Still held by Israelis after first Arab attacks in May
- ⇨ Invading Arab armies
- ✕✕ Heaviest fighting
- ➡ Jewish attacks at end of 1948
- – – – Palestine border

0 _____ 100 km
0 _____ 50 miles

In 1948–49 the Jews were fighting for national survival against apparently overwhelming odds. Something of their spirit is shown as they raise a home-made flag on the Red Sea shore, where Israel was soon to build the new port of Eilat.

they had just made and knowing that defeat meant its destruction. The isolated kibbutz of Yad Mordechai typified the Jewish spirit. It was attacked by 3,000 Egyptian troops, with tanks, heavy artillery and aircraft. An epic five-day seige followed in which a handful of settlers held out until they had lost over half their number. When at last the village fell the Egyptians burned what was left of it.

The only efficient Arab troops, Transjordan's Arab Legion, captured the eastern part, or Old City, of Jerusalem. Further north they and the Iraqis seemed about to cut Israel in two and reach the sea. Then, on 11 June, the United Nations mediator, the Swedish Count Bernadotte, managed to arrange a month's truce. During it, the Jews received money and weapons, and reorganized their forces. When fighting began they scored quick successes. There was another truce, but by now many Jews were confident of victory and impatient to finish the struggle. Stern Gang terrorists murdered Bernadotte, and when the final phase of the fighting began, the Jews drove their enemies back on all fronts except Jerusalem. The Arab alliance began to crumble. Abdullah of Transjordan took the lead in seeking a truce that allowed him to hold what his Arab Legion had won. By January 1949 Bernadotte's successor, the American diplomat Ralph Bunche, was able to arrange a general cease-fire.

The new state of Israel had won a considerable victory, though at a cost of 5,000 dead. It gained all of Galilee, with other smaller territories in addition to what the UN had allotted. The Middle East settled into a period of uneasy peace, and began to adjust to the presence of a very different nation in its midst.

Problems of 'Peace'

Though the Arab states had agreed to a cease-fire, they refused to make peace or even to recognize Israel's existence.

They resented Israel as a European outpost imposed upon the Arab world and sustained by American dollars. They continued the war by economic means, such as closing the Suez Canal to Israel's shipping. Israel retaliated by refusing to readmit the 700,000 Arabs who fled from their homes in the course of the war to become refugees in the camps beyond her borders.

The refugee problem was made worse by the fact that the surrounding Arab states were both unable and unwilling to

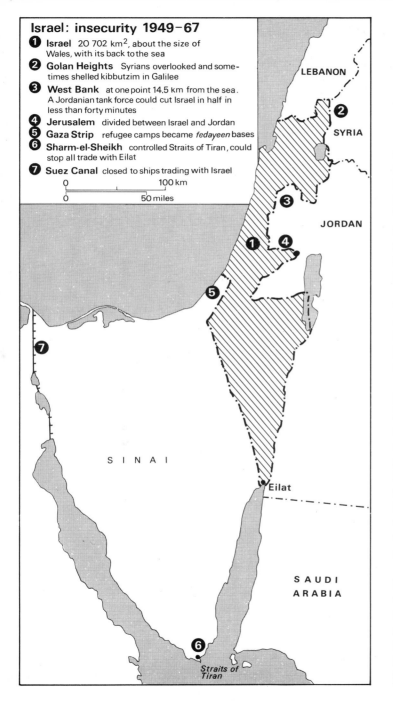

Israel: insecurity 1949–67

❶ Israel 20 702 km[2], about the size of Wales, with its back to the sea

❷ Golan Heights Syrians overlooked and sometimes shelled kibbutzim in Galilee

❸ West Bank at one point 14.5 km from the sea. A Jordanian tank force could cut Israel in half in less than forty minutes

❹ Jerusalem divided between Israel and Jordan

❺ Gaza Strip refugee camps became *fedayeen* bases

❻ Sharm-el-Sheikh controlled Straits of Tiran, could stop all trade with Eilat

❼ Suez Canal closed to ships trading with Israel

```
0              100 km
|--------|--------|
0        50 miles
```

LEBANON

SYRIA

JORDAN

SINAI

Eilat

SAUDI ARABIA

Straits of Tiran

absorb so many destitute people. Camps were set up in the Gaza Strip, held by Egypt, and the West Bank areas annexed by Transjordan, now renamed the Kingdom of Jordan. In their overcrowded misery resentment against Israel festered. The Palestinian Arabs became a people without a country, as the Jews had been, and pawns in the struggle between Israel and her neighbours. They were a constant threat both to Israel and to the stability of the countries that had unwillingly taken them in.

Israel would not allow the refugees to return to their homes without guarantees for her security from her neighbours. In any case, their abandoned homes and lands were soon taken by others, for in the first two years of her existence Israel took in more than half a million Jewish immigrants, from Europe and from the communities scattered through the Middle East.

Though the Palestinian flight made it possible for Israel to house so many immigrants, the doubling of its population in little more than three years brought David Ben-Gurion's government many problems. Theirs was a small country, with deserts, swamps and barren hills. It had to support a rapidly growing population unaccustomed to the hard, impoverished life of the Middle-Eastern farmer. It was poor in natural resources, with no coal or oil and few minerals of any kind. Yet there was an active trade-union movement demanding high wages and living standards. Israel needed to buy goods, and vital weapons, from the outside world; but she had little save citrus fruits to export in return.

The government set about schemes to develop agriculture (mainly through the kibbutzim) and industry, to cultivate wasteland and desert, to drain and irrigate, to build busy new towns, to provide machinery and good roads. They were remarkably successful, though Israel's exports remained less than half her imports. Money poured in to help development, from the USA and from overseas Jews, and also from Western Germany, whose government gave generously to Israel as

Arab refugees from Palestine 1948

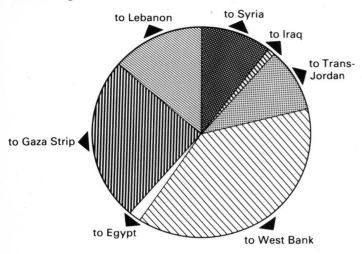

Jewish immigrants to Israel May 1948–51

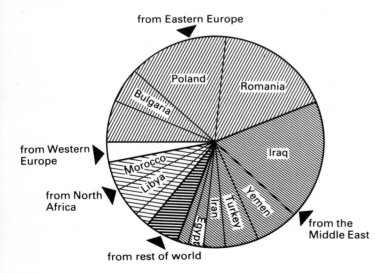

compensation for what the Nazis had done to the Jews.

Immigration produced social problems, but youth and the enthusiasm to build a new state and society overcame them. Education was expanded rapidly to fit people from diverse backgrounds for living together, and intensive courses in Hebrew helped give everyone a common language and culture. The army, in which all young men trained compulsorily, also included as many as a third of all young women and this helped towards social unity. But there remained deep divisions, particularly between Western Jews, well-educated and highly skilled, who ran Israel's government and industry, and Oriental Jews from the Middle-Eastern lands, mostly of simple peasant origin. These, known as 'Sephardic' Jews (though the word originally meant those from Spain and Portugal), were probably in a majority, yet they rarely reached higher education or top jobs. Israel developed as a very Westernized country, which emphasized its differences with its neighbours.

Israel's rapid progress was constantly threatened from outside. Her frontiers gave no security. North, south and east there were neighbours anxious to recover from the humiliation of 1948–49.

Key events

1946	Anglo–American Commission. King David Hotel explosion
1947	UN Partition Plan
1948	British withdrawal. Israel proclaimed
1948–49	Palestine War

4 Israel at bay 1949–67

Arab nationalism

The Arabs have always been a proud people. They felt bitter shame at their defeat, and resented the Western interference which had helped bring it about. But Arab pride had often gone hand-in-hand with self-deception, so that grand words took the place of well-directed action. As King Abdullah once said, 'the Arabs must give up daydreaming and apply themselves to reality'. Young Arab enthusiasts blamed their own leaders; the disaster must surely be an outcome of their inefficiency, slackness and treacherous collusion with the West. In the years after 1949, old rulers were rejected in favour of young and aggressive nationalists. Usually the revolutionaries who seized power came from the army, where the officers (who had often risen from peasant backgrounds) felt particularly humiliated by defeat and were impatient of old-fashioned leaders and bungling civilians. In the quarter-century after 1949 there were thirty successful revolutions and at least fifty unsuccessful attempts in the Arab world as one military chief replaced another. Parliamentary government, that cumbersome Western invention, did not seem workable to most Arabs; they preferred to follow a single dynamic leader. Only Lebanon among Arab states attempted Western-style democracy, and she faced enormous difficulties.

In Syria civilian government was overthrown by the army in 1949, and there were two more coups in the same year before a lasting soldier-dictator emerged. In Jordan King Abdullah was assassinated by a Palestinian fanatic in 1951, but his young grandson Hussein succeeded in keeping power with the support of his army and desert tribesmen. The most important revolution was in Egypt, where in 1952 a 'Free Officers' revolt took place. Its nominal leader, General Neguib, was soon replaced by the real master-mind, Colonel Gamal Abdel Nasser. The lazy, pleasure-loving King Farouk, who had been humiliated by the British and the Israelis, was allowed to sail away into exile with a fortune in Egyptian gold aboard his

Gamal Abdel Nasser, 1918–70, was son of a post office clerk in upper Egypt. Army officer, 1938, and soon joined a group of young officers plotting against the king. Upset by 1948 war disasters, master-minded 1952 plot which expelled king. At home, many reforms helped peasants and developed state socialism. In foreign affairs, failed to unite Arabs under his leadership against Zionism and British colonialism. Planned Aswan High Dam. 1956, nationalized Suez Canal, provoking war with Israel, Britain, France – military defeat but diplomatic victory. Militarily dependent on Russia. Humiliated by rapid defeat in 1967 war, but kept his popularity at home.

yacht. Then Egypt's new rulers set about the real business of revolution, and building their own kind of socialism. Parliament was dismissed and political parties abolished. Sweeping reforms broke up great estates and distributed land to the peasants. New industries and new schools were set up. Plans were made for a huge new dam at Aswan that would transform Egypt's economy. The British were persuaded to give up their military bases in the Suez Canal zone, and their armies finally left early in 1956 after seventy years in Egypt. They retained the right to return if the safety of the Canal were threatened.

Nasser and other new leaders soon realized that they could profit from the Cold War, then at its height. America and her allies feared the Soviet Union, and sought to encircle her with bases and alliances. Britain arranged the Baghdad Pact, link-

The creation of a Jewish state in Palestine resulted in at least 700,000 Arabs being driven from their homes to become refugees in camps around Israel's borders. Some were housed in official UN camps and helped by the UN Relief and Works Agency. Here young Arabs at a camp near Bethlehem face a future as landless exiles, dependant for food and medicine on international aid.

ing in alliance her remaining friends: Iraq, Iran, Turkey and Pakistan. Similarly, Communist Russia was only too ready to aid Middle-Eastern sympathizers, whether they were oil-rich capitalists or ambitious military dictators. When Arab leaders turned towards the USSR for arms or money, the USA tried either bribery or bullying to win them back. Some Arabs soon learned how best to exploit this situation.

Alliance and intrigue

The Arab refugees in camps around Israel's borders lived in a kind of limbo, fed, sheltered, given medical aid and education by the United Nations Relief and Works Agency (UNRWA). Some refugees found jobs, but these were generally the better educated, whose skills were in demand. Yasser Arafat, for example, worked as an engineer first in Egypt and later in Kuwait. For the majority, life in camps bred only discontent and a feeling that the world had forgotten them. In such a situation it was inevitable that many of the younger refugees would wish to fight to regain their land. Thus the problem of refugees produced the problem of terrorists. 'Freedom fighters', *fedayeen,* struck into Israel, and Israelis retaliated with reprisal raids on the villages which harboured them. With Gaza and the Sinai frontier in a constant turmoil of raid and reprisal, there could be no peace between Egypt and Israel. The UN truce supervisors noted 100,000 frontier violations between 1949 and 1967, though many of the early incidents involved refugees merely trying to return to their farms to collect possessions or pick the fruit from their trees.

Constant guerilla activities set both sides searching for arms and allies. Britain, France and the United States agreed in 1950 to limit arms supplies to the two sides, hoping to bring some stability to the region. But Israel, facing constant threats,

had developed a 'fortress mentality', and Ben-Gurion desperately needed a supply of up-to-date weapons. He found sympathizers in France who were prepared to ignore the arms agreement because they too regarded Nasser as a dangerous dictator who encouraged Algerian nationalists against French rule. In 1955 France supplied Israel with Mystère 4s, the best fighter aircraft in Europe.

The rocky fortress of Masada, defended to the death in AD 73 by Jewish rebels against Roman legions, came to symbolize Israel's determination to hold out at all costs against her encircling foes. The Israelis mounted a large-scale excavation, under Yigael Yadin, who was both a general and an archaeologist.

At the same time, Egypt sought arms from the Communist powers. After an Israeli attack on fedayeen bases in the Gaza strip had killed 36 Egyptian soldiers early in 1955, Nasser negotiated an arms deal with Czechoslovakia; the Russians and their allies were only too ready to respond if they could break into the Western hold on the Middle East. Egypt duly got eighty Mig 15 fighters, forty-five Ilyushin 28 bombers, and 115 of Russia's best battle tanks. Clearly these new weapons were for use against Israel, and the Jews were not slow to react.

Nasser's actions strengthened the position of the 'hawks' in Israel, leaders like Ben-Gurion and Moshe Dayan who wanted to strike first without waiting to be attacked. The hawks wanted to end the fedayeen raids that were making the frontier areas impossible for farmers, break the blockade that stopped ships using the Suez Canal and reaching the port of Eilat, and remove the constant threat from Russian bombers. Israel needed an ally, preferably one with long-range bombers to destroy Egypt's air-force on the ground. Britain, with Canberra bombers stationed in Cyprus, could carry out such a raid; but in 1955 Britain's pro-Arab position made it unlikely that she would help Israel. Events were to change Britain's attitude.

The Suez War

While President Nasser was getting military aid from the Communist world, he was also seeking economic aid from the West. The Aswan Dam and its electricity would transform Egypt's economy. The USA, Britain and the World Bank had agreed to finance it. When they heard of Nasser's dealings with the Communists, however, they decided to withdraw their offer. In July 1956, Nasser was told that he would get no money for his great project. His reaction was immediate and dramatic. On 26 July he nationalized the British- and French-owned Suez Canal Company, seized its assets and announced that it would in future be managed by Egyptians for Egypt's benefit.

For Britain in particular the news was like a bombshell. Britain still had imperial possessions and armies in the Far East, as well as a stake in Persian Gulf oil. She also had allies in the Middle East like Nuri-es-Said, leader of Iraq, a vital figure in the Baghdad Pact and an opponent of Nasser. By his action, the Egyptian leader was threatening British interests as well as undermining imperial prestige. He might offer compensation to shareholders and guarantee to keep the Canal open to all, but what he had done seemed illegal and dangerous. The British prime minister, Anthony Eden, saw Nasser as an ambitious Fascist dictator who must never be appeased as Hitler had been, as an ally of Russia and as an enemy to those Arab rulers who still supported Western policies.

Thus Britain came together with France and Israel to overthrow Nasser. What they needed was an excuse to start military action, and Israel agreed to provide it. On 23 and 24 October 1956 a secret meeting took place at Sèvres, just out-

Moshe Dayan, 1915–81. Born to immigrant parents at Degania, Palestine's first kibbutz. 1937, began military career, helping British army against Arabs. Haganah member, imprisoned by British 1939, but released and fought for them in Syria, 1941, where he lost his left eye. 1948, Haganah commander in Jerusalem. 1953–58, Israeli chief of staff, planned 1956 Sinai campaign. 1959, entered Knesset in Labour Party. 1967, minister of defence, planned brilliantly successful Six-Day War. 1973, criticised for lack of readiness in Yom Kippur War. 1977, foreign minister under Begin, and worked for peace settlement of 1979. Resigned in opposition to Begin's aggressive policy over Israeli West Bank settlements. A historian and archaeologist as well as Israel's favourite soldier.

Golda Meir, 1898–1978, born in the Ukraine, emigrated to USA, 1906. Trained as teacher, became a Zionist, went to Palestine 1921 with husband Morris Myerson. Joined a kibbutz and became prominent in Histadrut. A forceful spokesman for Zionism, she worked closely with Ben-Gurion as emissary to King Abdullah, USSR and USA. His minister of labour, 1949, and foreign minister, 1956. Prime minister, 1969–74. Tough and likable, she lost popularity after the 1973 war.

side Paris, at which the British, French and Israelis came to an agreement. Then the Israelis prepared their attack into Sinai, to crush the fedayeen and open the Gulf of Aqaba, secure in the knowledge that British bombers would eliminate danger from the Egyptian air force. The British and French, for their part, knew they would be given an excuse to take over the Canal, topple Nasser, and recover a base and influence in the Middle East.

On 29 October Israel launched her attack on Egypt when 395 paratroops, led by Ariel Sharon, landed at Mitla Pass in the heart of Sinai. Such unannounced lightning attacks were to become common in Middle-Eastern warfare. Moshe Dayan, Israel's chief of staff, aimed to create a threat to the Suez Canal and disrupt Egyptian defences. Britain and France, as arranged, promptly ordered both Israel and Egypt to withdraw their troops 16 km on each side of the Canal.

The Franco-British demand was plainly nonsense, since the Israelis were still nowhere near the Canal. Opinion throughout the world reacted violently against what seemed blatant aggression. The USA was particularly anxious not to be seen approving an imperialist attack on an independent Arab state. In the United Nations there were angry demands that the fighting must stop. Britain and France vetoed Security Council resolutions, but they could not stop the General Assembly calling for a cease-fire on 2 November. Defying the United Nations, British aircraft bombed Egypt's airfields, and a joint British and French invasion force landed beside the Canal.

However, Britain and France could not stand against the shocked world. Opinion in Britain itself was deeply divided, while Commonwealth leaders like Indian prime minister Nehru were very angry. Russia threatened to use missiles against London, but this was mere 'sabre-rattling', designed to impress the Arab world and distract attention from her own brutal suppression of Hungarian liberty. American economic pressure was much more important in forcing Eden to change his mind. Britain's trading partners feared that she might be unable to pay her way, and the pound lost value in world markets. Faced with complete collapse of their currency and trade, Britain and France gave way. Their troops had no

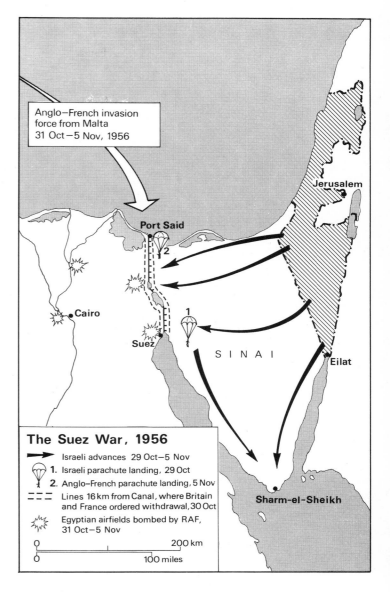

Anglo-French invasion force from Malta
31 Oct – 5 Nov, 1956

Jerusalem

Port Said

Cairo

Suez

S I N A I

Eilat

Sharm-el-Sheikh

The Suez War, 1956

➤ Israeli advances 29 Oct–5 Nov
1. Israeli parachute landing, 29 Oct
2. Anglo-French parachute landing, 5 Nov
- - - Lines 16 km from Canal, where Britain and France ordered withdrawal, 30 Oct
Egyptian airfields bombed by RAF, 31 Oct–5 Nov

0   200 km
0   100 miles

sooner landed and captured their first targets than they ceased fire on 6 November and prepared to withdraw.

The Suez fiasco showed how far Britain had declined as a world power and ended her leading part in Middle-Eastern affairs. Those Arabs who had resented British interference

Faced with Israeli and Anglo–French attacks, Nasser ordered the sinking of 50 concrete-filled ships to block the Suez Canal to all use. These are at the Canal's Port Said entrance.

were pleased to find themselves backed by world opinion, and were pleased with Russia's support. Arab rulers who still looked to Britain for friendship and help were left in difficulties. Hussein of Jordan had already sacked his British general and adviser, Sir John Glubb. Feisal II of Iraq and his pro-British prime minister Nuri-es-Said were killed in an army revolution in 1958, and Britain lost her bases in Iraq. The greatest danger seemed to be that Russia might step into Britain's place, and the United States, alarmed at this possibility, introduced the 'Eisenhower Doctrine' in 1958, offering support to Middle-Eastern states threatened by Communism. But Arab rulers, though ready to take Russia's money and weapons, were less willing to take her orders.

In Arab eyes Nasser emerged as a hero. He had wiped away the shame of military defeat (which could anyway be blamed on Israel's powerful and underhand allies) by his courage in confronting two great powers and winning a diplomatic vic-

tory. His prestige was high. He developed ambitious plans to unite the Arab world under his leadership but they made little headway in the face of other Arab rulers' suspicions.

Egypt kept the Canal and operated it smoothly. It remained closed to the Israelis. They had to withdraw from all their gains of the brief war. Their co-operation with Britain and France, two ex-colonial powers, made them suspect in the eyes of the Third World nations, who had only recently gained independence themselves and feared to lose it. Nevertheless, the Israelis had destroyed many fedayeen bases and when the international UN Emergency Force (UNEF) arrived to patrol the Sinai frontier, Israel had a chance to develop peacefully for a decade after 1956. The UNEF also supervised Sharm-el-Sheikh, controlling the Straits of Tiran at the mouth of the Gulf of Aqaba, ensuring free passage for ships trading with Israel's new port at Eilat.

The Six-Day War

In the ten years after the Suez War, the Arab world was split by civil war, insurrection and revolution. In Iraq the military dictator of 1958 soon gave place to another; both faced rebellions from their Kurdish subjects and quarrels with Syria. In Yemen there was civil war, with Egypt and Saudi Arabia interfering on opposite sides. President Nasser, though his plans for Arab unity came to nothing, continued to dominate Middle-Eastern politics. He enjoyed Russia's friendship and help in completing the Aswan High Dam and rebuilding his armed forces. To counter Russian influence, the USA openly supported Israel and the pro-western rulers of Lebanon and Jordan. Israel remained the only issue able to bring Arabs of all kinds together in co-operation.

Meanwhile, oil revenues brought another kind of revolution. Saudi Arabia and Kuwait, until 1945 among the world's poorest and most backward countries, were suddenly fabulously rich. Their oil-rich ruling classes could afford every kind of western luxury, though many of their people still lived the impoverished desert life they had for centuries. Linked from 1961 in the Organization of Petroleum Exporting Countries (OPEC), these lands were now treated with respect in world affairs. They were ready to finance the Arab struggle against Israel.

Israel had no such oil wealth. She had to live on the energy and ingenuity of her people, and on the generosity of overseas Jews and the United States government. In the early 1960's Israel began planning irrigation of the waterless Negev Desert in the South, and in 1964 an engineering plant started to pump water from the River Jordan for this purpose. This angered the Arabs, for the Kingdom of Jordan also depended on the river. They called a summit conference at Cairo which decided to divert two of the Jordan's tributaries in Lebanon and Syria, and to set up a unified military command against Israel. The conference also set up a 'Palestine Liberation

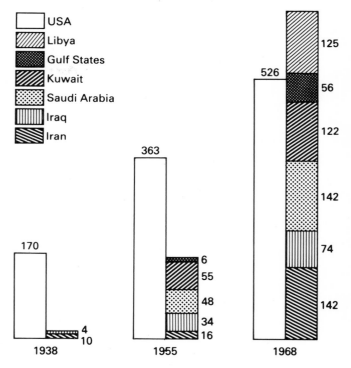

Oil: production in million metric tons
The USA was until the 1960s the world's largest oil producer; then the Middle East overtook it.

Legend:
- USA
- Libya
- Gulf States
- Kuwait
- Saudi Arabia
- Iraq
- Iran

1938: USA 170; Iran 4, 10

1955: USA 363; 6, 55, 48, 34, 16

1968: USA 526; 125, 56, 122, 142, 74, 142

Organization' (PLO) to bring together the refugees and their guerilla groups under a single ruling body, a government in exile. With the financial support of Saudi Arabia, the Arabs proposed 1970 as the provisional date for their war of liberation against the Zionists.

The activities of the PLO and of el Fatah, the guerilla force which joined it in 1968, were a continuing threat to Israel's security. El Fatah was headed by Yasser Arafat, who became chairman of the PLO in 1968. Under his leadership young guerillas, fired by a fierce hatred of everything Jewish, raided Israeli settlements killing indiscriminately. The Israelis retaliated against the 'breeding-grounds' of the guerillas, the refugee camps and border villages of Jordan and Syria. Once more the toll of innocent victims on both sides mounted. Perhaps the minds of the young suffered most, as they were battered from every side by violence and hatred. Arabs were

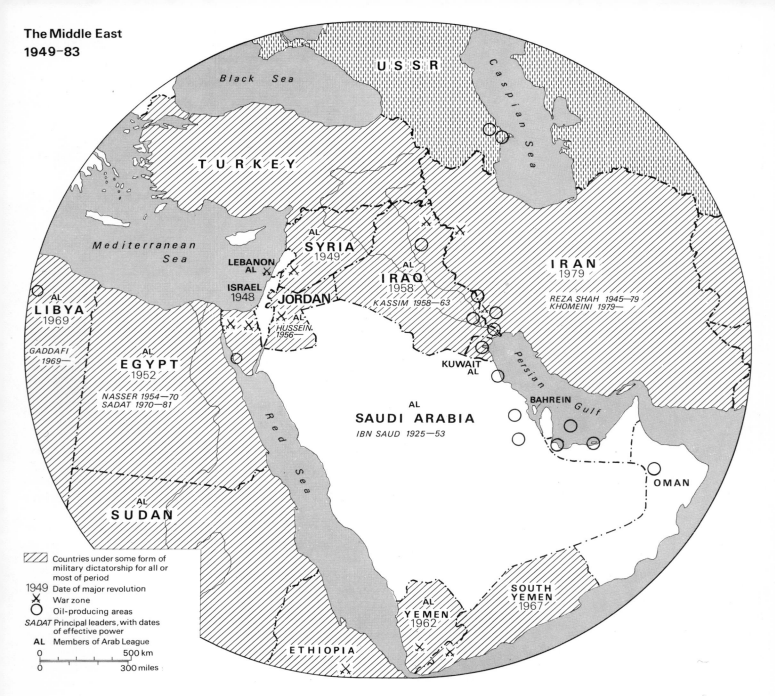

The Middle East
1949–83

USSR

Black Sea

Caspian Sea

T U R K E Y

Mediterranean Sea

AL
SYRIA
1949

LEBANON
AL

ISRAEL
1948

JORDAN

AL
HUSSEIN 1956—

AL
IRAQ
1958
KASSIM 1958–63

I R A N
1979

REZA SHAH 1945—79
KHOMEINI 1979—

AL
LIBYA
1969

GADDAFI 1969—

AL
EGYPT
1952

NASSER 1954–70
SADAT 1970–81

Red Sea

KUWAIT
AL

Persian Gulf

AL
SAUDI ARABIA

IBN SAUD 1925—53

BAHREIN

OMAN

AL
SUDAN

ETHIOPIA

AL
YEMEN
1962

SOUTH YEMEN
1967

Countries under some form of
military dictatorship for all or
most of period

1949 Date of major revolution

✕ War zone

◯ Oil-producing areas

SADAT Principal leaders, with dates
of effective power

AL Members of Arab League

0 _____ 500 km
0 _____ 300 miles

32

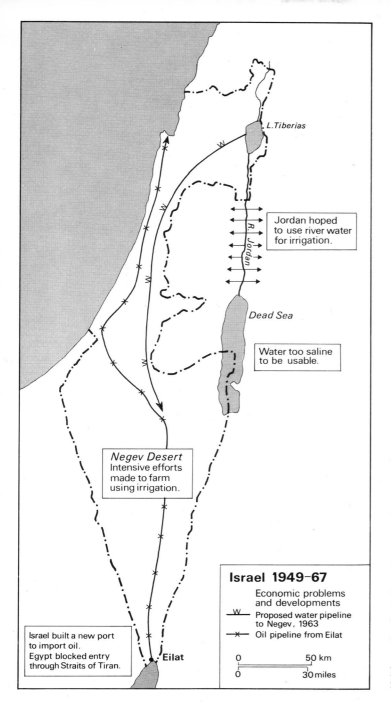

Israel 1949–67

Economic problems
and developments

—W— Proposed water pipeline
to Negev, 1963

—×— Oil pipeline from Eilat

0	50 km
0	30 miles

L.Tiberias

Jordan hoped
to use river water
for irrigation.

R. Jordan

Dead Sea

Water too saline
to be usable.

Negev Desert
Intensive efforts
made to farm
using irrigation.

Israel built a new port
to import oil.
Egypt blocked entry
through Straits of Tiran.

Eilat

Yasser Arafat, 1929–   , was
born in Jerusalem and
became an active leader of
exiled Palestinian students
at Cairo University.
Engineer in Egypt and
Kuwait. 1956, formed el
Fatah organization to
recover Palestine from
Zionists. 1968, Chairman of
PLO, organizing guerilla (or
terrorist) war. Led PLO away
from dependence on Egypt
and towards acceptance by
most of the world as a
government in exile. 1974,
addressed UN Assembly as
head of state. Made PLO a major force in Middle-Eastern
politics and a thorn in Israel's side. Driven from Jordan by
Hussein, 1970, and from southern Lebanon by Begin in 1982,
he lost the confidence of his followers. Many, supported by
Syria, turned against him in 1983.

told that they must destroy Israel, Jews that they were be-
sieged by an implacable enemy. Meanwhile Israel's army constantly demanded supplies of the latest aircraft and tanks to
counter Arab threats, and army leaders played an increasingly
important part in Israeli politics. One Israeli journalist, Boaz
Evron, noted in a Tel Aviv daily paper, 'The image of this
country, in which all talent is devoted to the battlefield, is that
of a country which thinks all solutions come from the tank and
the bulldozer, and this is the worst thing that can befall our
society.'

In 1966 and 1967 cross-border raids built up, and both sides
prepared for a showdown. Jordan and Syria, which suffered
most, taunted President Nasser with hiding behind the UN

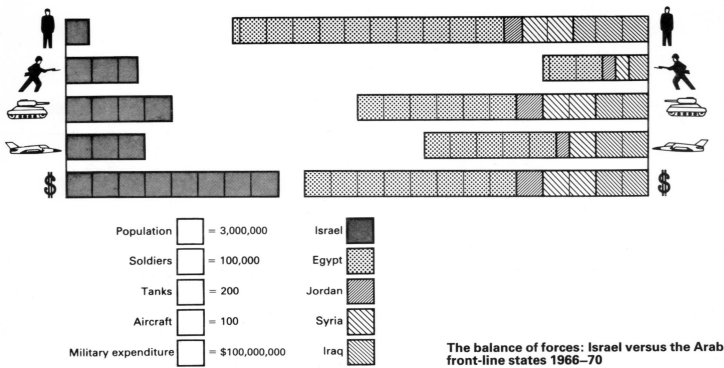

Population	□	= 3,000,000	Israel	■
Soldiers	□	= 100,000	Egypt	(dotted)
Tanks	□	= 200	Jordan	(diagonal)
Aircraft	□	= 100	Syria	(diagonal)
Military expenditure	□	= $100,000,000	Iraq	(diagonal)

The balance of forces: Israel versus the Arab front-line states 1966–70

Emergency Force patrolling his frontier. To maintain his standing in the Arab world Nasser was forced to demonstrate Egypt's strength and determination. Cairo radio and Egypttian newspapers launched a fresh barrage of insults and blood-curdling threats. Showy preparations for all-out war began. Nasser promised to 'liberate Palestine' and 'destroy Israel,' while the head of the PLO promised to help surviving Jews return to their native lands – but added that he thought 'none will survive'.

On 16 May 1967 Nasser ordered the UNEF to withdraw from Sinai, leaving Israel open to attack. The Egyptians occupied Sharm-el-Sheikh, stopping all traffic to Israel's port of Eilat. The Israelis decided that they must fight, and on 2 June appointed Moshe Dayan as defence minister. This time the Israelis determined that the dangerous frontiers left by the Palestine War must be permanently changed.

Israel faced the greatest threat to her existence since the early months of 1948. Her forces must meet attacks on three fronts simultaneously, from Syria, Jordan and Egypt. So the Israelis decided to make a pre-emptive strike rather than allow the Arabs to attack first. On the morning of 5 June the Israeli air force, flying west over the Mediterranean and then south, struck at ten Egyptian airfields. They destroyed first the runways and then as many Mig fighters as possible. In less than three hours over 300 Egyptian planes were destroyed, including thirty TU-16 bombers. At the same time, airfields in Syria, Jordan and Iraq were attacked. In all, Israel destroyed over 400 planes in a single morning for the loss of 26 of her own. The Jewish 'Blitzkrieg' settled the war's outcome in a few hours.

However, Dayan was eager to secure strategic frontiers before the United Nations could impose a cease-fire. Just half an hour after the first bombs fell the second stage of the Israeli plan was put into operation.

In Sinai, on Russian advice, the Egyptians occupied entrenched positions protected by sand dunes. The Israelis

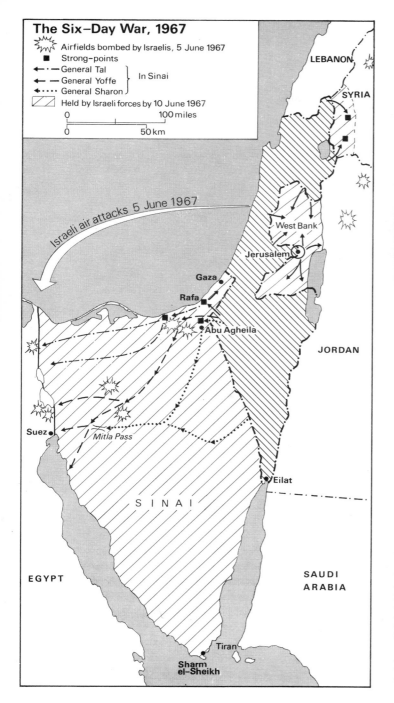

The Six-Day War, 1967

Airfields bombed by Israelis, 5 June 1967
■ Strong-points
◄—·— General Tal ⎫
◄— — General Yoffe ⎬ In Sinai
◄····· General Sharon ⎭
▨ Held by Israeli forces by 10 June 1967

0 ___ 100 miles
0 ___ 50 km

Israeli air attacks 5 June 1967

LEBANON
SYRIA
West Bank
Jerusalem
Gaza
Rafa
Abu Agheila
JORDAN
Suez
Mitla Pass
Eilat
S I N A I
EGYPT
SAUDI ARABIA
Tiran
Sharm el-Sheikh

In 1967 mastery of the air won by the Israelis in the first few hours of war enabled them to trap and destroy the retreating Egyptian armoured forces at the Mitla Pass.

attacked in three divisions. They used masses of tanks to crush opposition and lead the race forward, with commandos lifted by helicopter to by-pass the most dangerous strongholds. On the first day of fierce fighting they broke through at the main strong-points of Rafa and Abu Agheila, rushing westward along the coast and even through the dunes. The Egyptians fought back well at first despite their lack of air support; but Israeli dash overcame them. They started to retreat slowly, then turned and fled to get back to the Canal by way of the Mitla Pass. However, at Mitla the three Israeli forces encircled and trapped them. Aerial photographs in Western newspapers showed clearly what happened next as hundreds of Egyptian tanks and vehicles were caught in the pass by Israeli planes and destroyed or captured. The Israelis had conquered Sinai, and Sharm-el-Sheikh was taken without a fight.

At Jerusalem, on the West Bank, and on the Golan Heights, where Syria overlooked Israeli lowland settlements, there were similar spectacular successes. Israel had won vic-

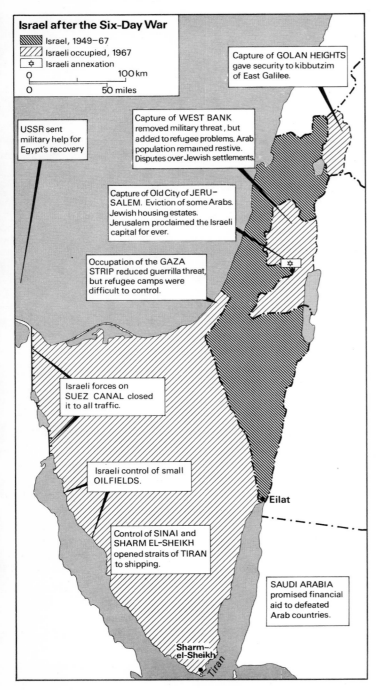

Israel after the Six-Day War

- **Israel, 1949-67**
- **Israeli occupied, 1967**
- ✡ **Israeli annexation**

0 — 100 km
0 — 50 miles

Capture of GOLAN HEIGHTS gave security to kibbutzim of East Galilee.

USSR sent military help for Egypt's recovery

Capture of WEST BANK removed military threat, but added to refugee problems. Arab population remained restive. Disputes over Jewish settlements.

Capture of Old City of JERU-SALEM. Eviction of some Arabs. Jewish housing estates. Jerusalem proclaimed the Israeli capital for ever.

Occupation of the GAZA STRIP reduced guerrilla threat, but refugee camps were difficult to control.

Israeli forces on SUEZ CANAL closed it to all traffic.

Israeli control of small OILFIELDS.

Control of SINAI and SHARM EL-SHEIKH opened straits of TIRAN to shipping.

SAUDI ARABIA promised financial aid to defeated Arab countries.

Eilat

Sharm-el-Sheikh

Tiran

tory in six days, one of the most complete victories in military history. Her troops had reached the defensible frontiers they needed. Nasser's army and air force had been destroyed, his canal was blocked, his Sinai oil wells were in Israeli hands. Jordan had lost the West Bank and Jerusalem, and had to absorb 100,000 new refugees. Deeply humiliated, Nasser and Hussein could only invent a story that the opening air raids were really the work of British and American planes from aircraft carriers in the Mediterranean. Such self-deception has often proved a major weakness among Arab leaders. Nevertheless, Israel could feel safe at last.

Key events

1952	Egyptian Revolution
1955	Baghdad Pact
1956	King Hussein dismissed Gen. Glubb. Suez War and UN intervention
1964	PLO set up
1967	Six-Day War

5 Peace and war 1967–83

A victory too great

After her astonishing success in the Six-Day War, Israel annexed East Jerusalem and occupied the Gaza Strip, the West Bank, Golan and Sinai, some 28,000 square miles in all, or more than three times her own original territory. Israelis believed that they could now use this territory for bargaining and could force the Arab states to make peace. However, the Arabs had lost too much. Their defeat was so humiliating that they could not negotiate with Israel as equals. Egypt in particular needed to regain her pride.

Once again Arab leaders met, and at Khartoum agreed not to recognize Israel, negotiate or make peace. Saudi Arabia and Kuwait undertook to make good financially the losses suffered by Egypt and Jordan. Russia began re-arming Egypt. Nasser seemed to be slipping more and more towards complete dependence on the USSR, and this alarmed the United States, who promptly re-armed Israel. The confrontation of the two super-powers posed a direct threat to world peace, and they recognized it. The USA led the way in an urgent search for a peaceful solution to the Middle East's problems. Russia did not obstruct her, and even President Nasser was now ready to listen. So was King Hussein, who arranged meetings with Israeli ministers to discuss future arrangements.

But if Egypt and Jordan were showing signs of moderation, other Arab countries as well as the Palestinians remained bitter and violent. Constant propaganda and indoctrination continued, and any book or film with the slightest taint of Jewishness was banned.

The Arab states had the sympathy of the United Nations, where Third World countries now predominated; but above all everyone wanted a permanent, peaceful settlement. In November 1967 the Security Council passed a resolution condemning Israel's acquisition of territory by force. Resolution 242/67 went on to require Israel's withdrawal and suggested a settlement that would include recognition of Israel by the Arabs and a fair deal for the Palestinians. The UN Special Representative, Gunnar Jarring, spent much time trying to win Arab and Jewish support for the principles of 242/67 with little success, and by 1970 attitudes had hardened. Fighting flared up once again with a long-range artillery bombardment across the Suez Canal, in what Nasser called a 'War of Attrition' to wear Israel down.

Egypt regains her pride

In 1970 President Nasser suddenly died and was succeeded by his close colleague in the 'Free Officers' movement, Anwar

Anwar es-Sadat, 1918–81, of peasant origin, became an army officer. Hating British interference and royal corruption, he was imprisoned for links with Nazi spies, 1942, and assassination plot, 1945. Returned to army, 1950, co-operating in Nasser's 'Free Officers' revolt, 1952. Held various posts as 'Nasser's poodle', 1952–70, then succeeded him as president, outmaneuvring rivals. Ended Nasser's dependence on Russian advisers and friendship, co-operating with USA. Modified Nasser's form of socialism, seeking practical economic progress, but failed to achieve it. In 1977 his bold visit to Israel forced Begin to talk peace and led to Camp David agreements, 1978, and Washington Treaty, 1979. Attacked by Arab and Islamic enthusiasts at home and abroad, and assassinated 1981, much mourned by the West.

Egyptian soldiers stormed across the Suez Canal to attack the Israeli Bar-Lev line. The attack was carried out with great skill, using the latest Russian equipment including water cannons to break the sand defences, and the Israeli defenders were taken by surprise. The myth of Israeli invincibility was broken.

es-Sadat. Sadat, though outwardly loyal to Nasser's policies, had his own ideas of Egypt's needs. He was prepared to seek capital abroad to develop Egypt's industries and encourage enterprise, even if it meant a move away from socialism and dependence on Russia. He soon found himself under Russian and American pressure to reach agreement with Israel and thus end uncertainty in the Middle East. But he had no wish to negotiate with Israel from a position of weakness, and when Russian advisers questioned his warlike preparations in 1972 he ordered them out of his country.

In planning a new war, Sadat was calculating cleverly. Both America and Russia publicly maintained that Israel should give up her 1967 gains, though the Israelis refused to do so without Arab guarantees of their security. Sadat hoped to strike Israel a sharp blow that would shock her into negotiating, and also force the great powers to intervene. They would then impose the fair settlement they favoured to secure a stable Middle East, so even if Egypt suffered defeat the Israelis would be compelled to withdraw. Since Israel was

already establishing settlements in Sinai, the Gaza Strip and the West Bank, it seemed ever less likely that she would willingly surrender them. Sadat had to strike soon and swiftly.

In September 1973 Sadat concluded a secret agreement with Syria for a joint attack. It was planned to take place on Yom Kippur, the Day of Atonement, when all Jews were praying and fasting. The attack took the Israelis completely by surprise, as they had so often surprised others. On 6 October a massive Egyptian air attack struck the Bar-Lev line beyond the Suez Canal, while commandos and 500 tanks quickly followed to break through and overwhelm its Israeli defenders. Israeli aircraft counter-attacking met mobile surface-to-air (SAM) missiles, and many were lost. Having scored opening successes the Egyptians, in answer to appeals from the Syrians (whose own attack was running into difficulties) began to move inland. This was a mistake, and they were repulsed by Israeli armoured forces. Then, on 15 October General Sharon began a daring counter-thrust across the Canal between two Egyptian armies. For a week the two sides tangled in fierce

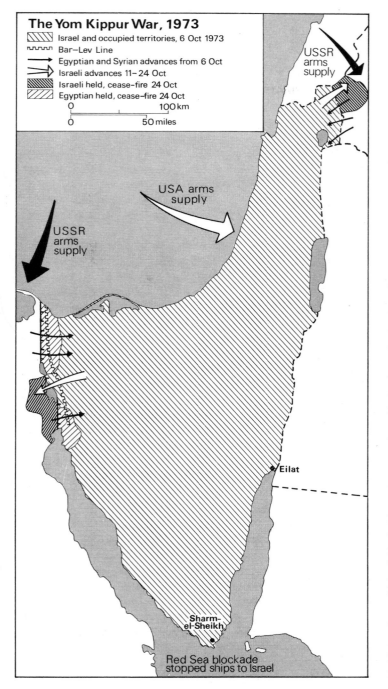

The Yom Kippur War, 1973

- ⬚ Israel and occupied territories, 6 Oct 1973
- ∿∿∿ Bar–Lev Line
- → Egyptian and Syrian advances from 6 Oct
- ⇒ Israeli advances 11– 24 Oct
- ⬚ Israeli held, cease–fire 24 Oct
- ⬚ Egyptian held, cease–fire 24 Oct

0   100 km

0   50 miles

USSR arms supply

USA arms supply

USSR arms supply

Eilat

Sharm-el-Sheikh

Red Sea blockade stopped ships to Israel

fighting. The Israelis won the battle of the Chinese Farm and were able to push on to the outskirts of Cairo before a cease-fire was agreed and the war ended on 24 October.

The Yom Kippur War had lasted less than three weeks, but it transformed the Middle East situation. The Egyptian crossing of the Canal and break-through was the success they needed to regain their pride. The Israelis too could pride themselves on their speedy recovery and on Sharon's masterstroke; on both fronts they had been able to press well into enemy territory. But they had faced unpleasant surprises. In Golan SAM missiles had shot down thirty Israeli planes on the first day, while hand-held 'Strella' missiles hit many more though they destroyed rather fewer. In Sinai Israelis met enemy soldiers apparently carrying suitcases – the portable 'Sagger' missiles which knocked out many Israeli tanks. This was a new kind of warfare. Israel's air superiority was endangered, and her occupied territories were no effective buffer against a missile-armed enemy.

The 1973 war showed the Arab world that it had another weapon, previously unsuspected. The Arab oil producers in OPEC banded together, threatening to cut back supplies by 5% and raise prices unless the Western world accepted Arab demands. The Gulf producers raised their prices by 70%. Saudi Arabia cut output by 10% and imposed a total ban on oil for the USA and the Netherlands, the countries most obviously friendly towards Israel. The European Economic Community was persuaded to express its sympathy for the Palestinian cause. The West had been hit where it hurt most, in the pocket; and Arab oil policies helped to start a long period of world economic difficulty and trade recession.

The war also underlined the danger of great power confrontation. The USA flew in massive quantities of arms to help Israel, while the USSR aided Egypt. At one moment it was feared that the Russians were actually supplying their ally with nuclear weapons. Such dangers must be averted, and the loss

of Saudi oil added to the urgency. Henry Kissinger, the US secretary of state, began a new peace mission, with Russian approval.

Peace between Israel and Egypt

In November 1977 President Sadat, once Israel's most dangerous enemy, flew to Jerusalem and addressed the *Knesset*, Israel's parliament. A month later the Israeli prime minister, Menachem Begin, hitherto a bitter opponent of compromise with the Arabs, returned his visit. Amazingly, peace seemed in sight between enemies who for thirty years had torn the Middle East apart.

Sadat was a realist. He accepted that Israel existed and had a right to security. He knew that his own country, with a fast-growing population and few resources, facing growing economic difficulties, could no longer stand heavy military expenditure and take part in a mad arms race. Any settlement that regained the lands Israel occupied was better, and far less costly, than continued conflict and instability.

Henry Kissinger, tirelessly flying round the Middle-Eastern capitals on his 'shuttle-diplomacy' missions of 1974 and 1975, had prepared the way. Though Jewish himself, he won Egyptian confidence by arranging a Geneva peace conference to disentangle the two armies facing each other warily in Sinai, and persuading the Israelis to draw back from the Canal. In Golan, too, Kissinger persuaded Syrians and Israelis to disengage. His efforts satisfied Saudi Arabia enough to get America's oil supplies restored, but they rather upset the watchful Russians as America seemed to be regaining friends and prestige.

Kissinger's strenuous efforts produced one concession after another. Sadat allowed Israeli cargoes through the Suez Canal when, at long last, it reopened; and he renounced war as a means of dealing with Israel. Israel returned the Sinai oilfields and withdrew from the Mitla Pass. Such gestures alarmed

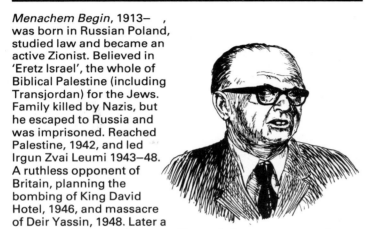

Menachem Begin, 1913–   , was born in Russian Poland, studied law and became an active Zionist. Believed in 'Eretz Israel', the whole of Biblical Palestine (including Transjordan) for the Jews. Family killed by Nazis, but he escaped to Russia and was imprisoned. Reached Palestine, 1942, and led Irgun Zvai Leumi 1943–48. A ruthless opponent of Britain, planning the bombing of King David Hotel, 1946, and massacre of Deir Yassin, 1948. Later a member of Knesset, in opposition to Labour governments. 1973, formed right-wing Likud alliance, and won 1977 election. As prime minister, 1977–83 accepted agreement with Egypt, but insisted on developing West Bank Israeli settlements, annexed Golan, and launched Lebanon War, 1982.

some Israelis. Early in 1977, for the first time in the country's history, the moderate socialists lost an election and a 'hawkish' right-wing government came to power headed by Menachem Begin. Begin held that the West Bank was an integral part of 'Eretz Israel', not an occupied territory, that to risk allowing it to become a PLO base was suicidal, and that Jewish settlement must be encouraged. Nevertheless, when Sadat suddenly proclaimed his willingness to visit his old enemy, Begin could hardly reject his gesture.

Sadat was endangering his standing in the Arab world. Extremists like Colonel Gaddafi of Libya were quick to condemn him, but outside the Middle East opinion welcomed and admired his bold move; the admiration was later shown in the

award of Nobel peace prizes to Sadat and Begin. But negotiations for a detailed peace settlement soon broke down, and the United States had to step in once more. This time the initiative came from President Carter, who invited both leaders to his holiday lodge at Camp David in Maryland. In September 1978 he persuaded them to accept two agreements:

A Framework for Peace in the Middle East, in which the West Bank and the Gaza Strip were to gain full self-government, and there would be no new Israeli settlements.

An Israeli–Egyptian Peace, under which Egypt would regain all Sinai over a three-year period, but agree to limit its military forces there.

Important issues were left out of the Camp David agreements: the PLO, Jerusalem and Golan. Most ominous of all, Begin would not agree to a permanent freeze on Jewish settlements in the occupied West Bank. This meant certain future trouble. But for the moment Carter seemed to have scored a triumphant breakthrough. His ceaseless efforts helped to overcome opposition from Israelis reluctant to give up their conquered territory, and on 26 March 1979 Egypt and Israel signed their treaty in Washington. By May Israel had begun withdrawal from Sinai, and completed the handover in 1982, though her army had to evict settlers and demolish newly built towns in the face of hard-line protests. Israel had traded occupied territory for guarantees of peace and security. Sadat had won for Egypt the immense practical benefit of peace and the return of her lost lands, but only by sacrificing his position and influence in the Arab world, where he was widely denounced for treachery to the Palestinian cause. Sadat's assassination by Muslim extremists in October 1981 brought no change in Egyptian policy. But his hopes of securing a general settlement of Arab–Israeli relations were not realised, and the

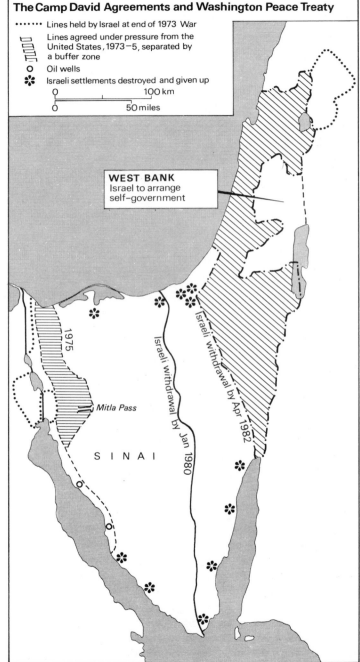

The Camp David Agreements and Washington Peace Treaty

- ⋯⋯⋯ Lines held by Israel at end of 1973 War
- Lines agreed under pressure from the United States, 1973–5, separated by a buffer zone
- ○ Oil wells
- ✽ Israeli settlements destroyed and given up

0   100 km
0   50 miles

WEST BANK
Israel to arrange self-government

1975

Mitla Pass

S I N A I

Israeli withdrawal by Jan 1980

Israeli withdrawal by Apr 1982

Colonel Muammar al Gaddafi
(or Qaddafi), 1942–
was born in a Libyan desert tent, became an army officer and led army seizure of power in 1969. Became head of armed forces and dictator. Made shrewd use of Libyan oil wealth to bargain with the West, and to build state socialism in Libya. A passionate believer in Islam and Libya, aggressive and excitable, he has fallen out with most of his neighbours and world powers.

other half of the Camp David agreement remained a dead letter, while Jews and Palestinians faced each other as stubbornly as ever. By 1981 there were 130 Jewish settlements in the occupied territories, while Jewish housing estates and evictions of Arabs, as well as Knesset decrees, had turned Jerusalem into an inalienably Israeli city. Facing this, Colonel Gaddafi and other Arab leaders constantly called for a military solution as the only way to achieve lasting peace in the Middle East.

The PLO and the Lebanon War

As Israel's southern border became stable and secure, the activities of the PLO threatened her from the north. The Palestine Liberation Organization reached a peak of influence in the 1970s, when it broke away from its Arab sponsors, ceased to be simply a weapon in their hands for use against

Israel, and developed policies of its own. The Palestinians were a new nation, formed in reaction against the Zionist invaders of their land, and their struggle made them bitterly aware of their separate identity. Israel naturally distrusted the PLO, since it existed solely to oppose Israeli nationhood.

Within the Arab world, and within the PLO itself, there were divisions between those who sought to reclaim all Palestine and expel the Jews, and those who hoped only for a Palestinian state in the occupied territories.

The Arab defeat of 1967, and Arab acceptance of Resolution 242/67 (which treated the Palestinians as 'refugees' rather than as a nation) showed the Palestinians they could not rely on their allies. Some, like the Popular Front for the Liberation of Palestine (PFLP) led by George Habash, turned to new forms of terrorism to attract world attention to their existence and fate. They linked with other terrorist groups such as the IRA and the Japanese Red Brigade, and staged a series of bloody incidents, usually directed against Israeli or Western aircraft. In 1970 their hi-jackings reached a peak when the PFLP seized four air-liners, flew them to Jordan, burned the planes and held the passengers hostage. Such outrages forced King Hussein to discipline his unruly guests before Israel and the Western powers intervened to do so, and in 'Black September' he turned on the PLO and crushed their organization in Jordan. Hussein "killed more Palestinians in 11 days than Israel could kill in 20 years," said Moshe Dayan with satisfaction. But the PLO fighters found new homes in Lebanon, where the small army was quite unable to do as Hussein had done and the people were already deeply divided. Terrorist attacks went on. In 1972 the group calling itself 'Black September' seized 11 athletes of the Israeli Olympic team at Munich and killed them during a subsequent rescue attempt. In 1976 the PFLP hi-jacked a French air-liner whose 247 passengers included 61 Israelis and took it to Entebbe in Uganda. On that occasion Israeli commandos carried out a hazardous but brilliantly successful rescue. In general, these outrages achieved the desired effect, making a horrified world aware of Palestinian demands, as they had been made aware of those of the Zionists in the 1940s. Arab governments accepted the PLO as an equal in 1974, and Yasser Arafat went to New York to address the UN General Assembly as a visiting head of state. The Palestine problem remained. The Palestinian people refused to disappear conveniently, just as Israel had refused to disappear after 1948. By 1975 there were some three million Palestinian Arabs, half under Israeli rule, 750,000 in Jordan, 400,000 in Lebanon and 200,000 in Syria.

Israel could do little but counter terrorism by terrorism. Murder squads were used to pick off PLO leaders around the world. More savage and indiscriminate were the retaliatory

King Hussein ibn Talal, 1935– , was born in Transjordan while his grandfather was Emir, and succeeded as King of Jordan after Abdullah's murder, 1951, and his insane father's abdication, 1952. Depended heavily on British and US military and financial support, but was forced by Arab opinion to sack his British C-in-C, General Glubb, 1956. Despite constant criticism from Arab extremists, and having to walk a tight-rope between Israeli and Arab pressures, clung to power with the aid of his army. Crushed PLO in Jordan, 1970.

raids against the unfortunate state of Lebanon. In 1968 a raid destroyed 13 Arab aircraft at Beirut airport. Subsequently a series of devastating raids by land, sea and air struck at Palestinian camps, inevitably killing women and children as well as PLO fighters. Lebanon's long ordeal was beginning.

Lebanon, carved out of Syria under the French Mandate and given independence in 1943, was one of the richest Arab states. Its population was a confusing mixture of Arabs and Europeans, Christians and Muslims (both sub-divided into many sects: Maronite, Orthodox and Armenian; Druse, Sunni and Shiite) speaking various dialects of Arabic, French and English. There were prosperous cities where business men (mostly Westernised and mostly Christian) made money from trade, banking and tourism; and there were peasant farmers and herdsmen in the mountains who were mostly Muslim. Lebanon had a democratic constitution, and a parliament that reflected the 6:5 Christian majority of the population which had existed under the French Mandate, with a president who was always Christian and a prime minister always Muslim. By the 1960s that balance had changed so that Muslims probably outnumbered Christians and sought more political power.

Into this unstable community came the Palestinian Arabs to tip the balance further towards the Muslims. A civil war broke out in 1975 as the PLO threw its weight on the Muslim side. A Christian military force, the Phalange, now extended its activities to drive out the Palestinians. But the war was many-sided. Each group, whether motivated by religion, political principle, nationalism, or greed and ambition, had its own private army. In 1976 Syria stepped in, attempting to restore order, but only added to the confusion. Beirut was badly battered, many of its great tourist hotels burning wrecks, while Lebanon was unofficially divided among the various groups.

All this alarmed the Israelis, who saw their PLO enemies establishing a secure position in their war-torn neighbour. They hoped to keep the area just over the frontier and south of the Litani River as a buffer zone, and supported a Christian private army there, supplying it with weapons and medical aid. Then, in 1977, Begin came to power, grumbling that Beirut was the centre for international terrorism. In March 1978, as peace moves progressed over her southern frontier, Israel invaded Lebanon in reprisal for attacks on Galilee villages and to bolster her Christian allies. The arrival of United Nations troops prevented a fresh war between Israel and Syria, and the Israelis withdrew.

Ariel Sharon, 1928–   , was born in Israel and became an energetic Haganah soldier under Ben-Gurion. Commanded reprisal raids on Palestinian camps, 1953–56, and parachute landing near Mitla Pass in 1956. Studied law at Tel Aviv, then headed brigade group in Six-Day War, leading dash across Sinai. In Yom Kippur War, 1973, led successful counter-attack across Suez Canal. Helped Begin form right-wing alliance, 1973. 1977, minister of agriculture, responsible for Israeli settlements in occupied territories. 1981, minister of defence, and planned 1982 invasion of Lebanon. Blamed for allowing Beirut massacres of Palestinians, 1982, but kept Begin's support and post in Cabinet.

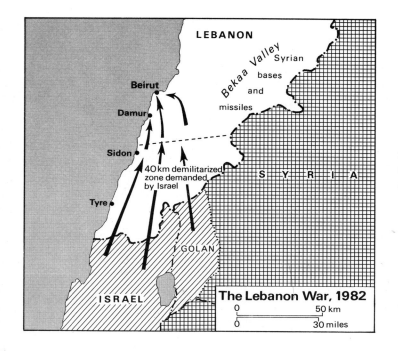

LEBANON

Bekaa Valley Syrian
bases
and
missiles

Beirut

Damur

Sidon

40 km demilitarized
zone demanded
by Israel

S Y R I A

Tyre

GOLAN

ISRAEL

The Lebanon War, 1982

0 _____ 50 km

0 _____ 30 miles

However, Israel could not ignore the growing domination of Lebanon by Palestinians, and her Christian friends seemed in ever-growing danger, while the UN force could do little to check terrorism. Israeli opinion was restive, for many were disappointed by the loss of the Sinai settlements. In 1981 Begin appointed as his defence minister Ariel Sharon, whose aggressiveness and drive had done much to win the Sinai campaigns of 1967 and 1973. In June 1982, a Palestinian attack severely injured the Israeli ambassador in London. This was the prelude to a new outbreak of fighting. The Israelis launched 'Operation Peace for Galilee', a full-blown invasion of Lebanon. Begin and defence minister Sharon declared their intention of driving the PLO fighters 40 km back from the Israeli frontier, and within five days this line was reached; but no halt was called. The Israeli leaders were going to settle Lebanon's problems by force and break the PLO's power. It was a savage and destructive war. The cities of Tyre, Sidon and Damur were devastated, many civilians were killed and many thousands left homeless. Syrian aircraft and missile systems were destroyed in ferocious fighting when they tried to

intervene. Sharon's purpose became clear as Israeli troops closed in on Beirut, where 8,000 PLO fighters were trapped along with half a million civilians.

The Lebanon War was the most long-drawn-out and unpleasant conflict in the thirty-five violent years of Israel's history. It produced uncertainty in the minds of many Jews. Previous wars had been fought in self-defence; how could this act of aggression be justified?

The ten-week siege of West Beirut, with Israeli bombs and shells pounding houses, flats, hotels and hospitals into ruins, was watched by horrified television viewers all over the world. Even President Reagan of the United States openly criticized Israel's stubbornly aggressive attitude. He sent a special representative, Philip Habib, who was able to hammer out a cease-fire. An international force of French, Italian and American troops supervised the evacuation of PLO fighters from Beirut and their dispersal among nine neighbouring Arab states.

As the international force withdrew, the city of Beirut was occupied by Israeli forces, the first Arab capital to fall to what some described as Israeli imperialism. On Friday 17 September, Christian Phalangists and members of Major Saad Haddad's Christian Militia entered the Palestinian camps of Chatila and Sabra and carried out an appalling massacre of helpless men, women and children. By the next day over a thousand Palestinians had been murdered and it was clear that the Israeli forces had known of the massacres and had not acted to prevent them. This still further tarnished the reputation of Israel and won more sympathy for the Palestinian cause than decades of terrorism had.

Israel had succeeded in punishing her bitterest enemies and scattering the PLO, but at a terrible cost. She remained deeply divided; her friends abroad were shocked by her conduct, and within Israel shame and outrage was widespread. Civilians and soldiers openly demonstrated their disgust over the

Israeli air raids and shelling on West Beirut took a savage toll of lives and property. As the PLO fighters were forced into an enclave in the city bombardment became more indiscriminate. Here dense black smoke pours from the scene of an explosion, while ambulances wait to take the injured to hospitals, but these offered no safety from bombs and shells.

heavy-handed policies of Begin and Sharon. Never before had the Israelis been so doubtful, divided and embittered by their government's conduct. Nevertheless, Begin remained in power until ill-health forced his resignation in 1983. His successor, Shimon Peres, took office with a pledge to bring unity to the divided nation.

During 1983, the situation in Lebanon remained chaotic.

The country was torn apart by civil war and by the efforts of rival peace-keeping forces from Syria, Israel, and several western countries, including the United States and Britain. The violent clashes of these groups, sometimes involving warships, aircraft, artillery and suicidal bomb attacks, seemed likely to transform Lebanon's civil war into a major international crisis. Then, in early 1984, the Western powers gave up the job of maintaining peace in the devastated country and withdrew their forces. During the following year, Israel began a gradual withdrawal of its troops, leaving Syria as the dominant influence within Lebanon. The destructive civil war continued, however, and Lebanon's future seemed bleak.

In the mid-1980's, the major conflict between Israel and the Arabs remained unresolved. The outside world still faced

By January 1984 the end was in sight for the international peace-keeping forces in Lebanon. Here a British helicopter waits to evacuate British nationals from beseiged Beirut. In the foreground a US marine stands guard.

the problem of checking Israel's aggressiveness and at the same time meeting her need for security. Somehow an internationally acceptable plan for the future of the Middle East had to be found. Almost everyone agreed that the Palestinians had a right to a West Bank homeland but disagreed over its nature. The Arabs had proposed at Fez in 1982 that it be an independent state. The West's view, as put forward by President Reagan, called for partial self-government for Palestinians on the West Bank, but the Israelis were not prepared to give up their own control of the area. As always, the Palestinians remained a serious stumbling block to Middle Eastern peace. The rival nation brought into being by Israel's own birth would not go away.

Key events

1970	Nasser's 'War of Attrition'. Black September: King Hussein crushed PLO.
1973	Yom Kippur War
1976	Entebbe hi-jacking and rescue
1977	Sadat's visit to Jerusalem
1978	Camp David agreements
1979	Washington Treaty between Egypt and Israel
1982	Sinai evacuation completed. Lebanon War.

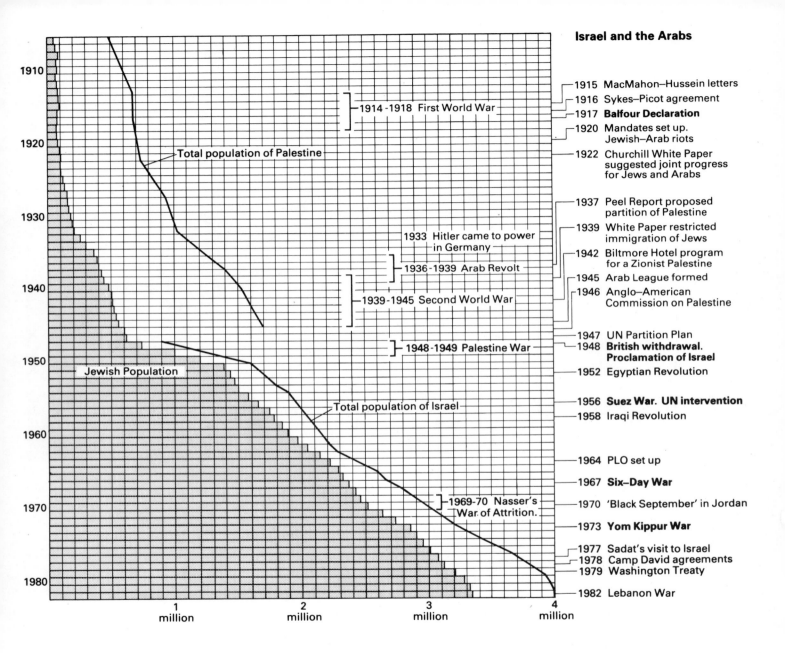

Israel and the Arabs

1915 MacMahon–Hussein letters
1916 Sykes–Picot agreement
1917 Balfour Declaration
1920 Mandates set up.
Jewish–Arab riots
1922 Churchill White Paper
suggested joint progress
for Jews and Arabs

1937 Peel Report proposed
partition of Palestine
1939 White Paper restricted
immigration of Jews
1942 Biltmore Hotel program
for a Zionist Palestine
1945 Arab League formed
1946 Anglo–American
Commission on Palestine

1947 UN Partition Plan
**1948 British withdrawal.
Proclamation of Israel**
1952 Egyptian Revolution

1956 Suez War. UN intervention
1958 Iraqi Revolution

1964 PLO set up
1967 Six–Day War
1970 'Black September' in Jordan

1973 Yom Kippur War
1977 Sadat's visit to Israel
1978 Camp David agreements
1979 Washington Treaty
1982 Lebanon War

1914 -1918 First World War

Total population of Palestine

1933 Hitler came to power
in Germany
1936 -1939 Arab Revolt

1939 -1945 Second World War

1948 -1949 Palestine War

Jewish Population

Total population of Israel

1969-70 Nasser's
War of Attrition.

1910
1920
1930
1940
1950
1960
1970
1980

1
million
2
million
3
million
4
million

Index

Acknowledgments

The author and publisher would like to thank the following for permission to reproduce illustrations:

front cover, p. 46 Camera Press; title page, pp. 20, 22, 35, 40 Israel Government Press Office; pp. 9, 26, 30 BBC Hulton Picture Library; pp. 10, 19 Central Zionist Archives; p. 27 Werner Braun; p. 38 Embassy of Arab Republic of Egypt; p. 47 Middle East Photographic Archive (photographer Liz Sly).

Diagrams by Gecko Studio Services
Maps by Reg Piggott
Portrait drawings by Ian Newsham

front cover: *A shipload of Jewish refugees arrives at their promised land. In the first 20 years after the creation of Israel in 1948, 1.3 million Jews entered the country. The dream of two thousand years was at last realized: Jews had a home of their own.*

back cover: *Which way now? Lebanese children stand amidst the ruins of Sidon after Israeli bombardment in June 1982. For the people of the Middle East 30 years of Arab-Israeli hostility had scarred the whole region.*

title page: *Early Jewish settlers set out to make a fertile land in the Palestinian desert. Here in 1910, pioneers work on the site of the future city of Tel Aviv, now the second biggest city in Israel.*

The Cambridge History Library

The Cambridge Introduction to History
Written by Trevor Cairns

The Cambridge Topic Books
General Editor Trevor Cairns

Lerner Publications Company
241 First Avenue North, Minneapolis, Minnesota 55401